CABINETMAKING

CABINET-MAKING

PAUL HAYNIE

Cabinetmaking Instructor
Atlanta Area Technical School
Atlanta, Georgia

PRENTICE-HALL, INC., Englewood Cliffs, New Jersey

Library of Congress Cataloging in Publication Data

Haynie, Paul   (date)
    Cabinetmaking.

    Includes index.
    SUMMARY: Gives step-by-step instructions for building
cabinets, from rough lumber to installation, with
emphasis on kitchen cabinets.
        1. Cabinet-work.   2. Kitchen cabinets.   1. Cabinet-
work.   2. Kitchen cabinets.   I. Title.
TT197.H37   684.1'6   75-2156
ISBN   0-13-110239-7

Cover photos courtesy of Del-Mar Cabinets, Atlanta, Georgia

Printed in the United States of America

10   9

Prentice-Hall International, Inc., *London*
Prentice-Hall of Australia, Pty. Ltd., *Sydney*
Prentice-Hall of Canada, Ltd., *Toronto*
Prentice-Hall of India Private Limited, *New Delhi*
Prentice-Hall of Japan, Inc., *Tokyo*
Prentice-Hall of Southeast Asia (PTE.) LTD., *Singapore*

CONTENTS

v

PREFACE

In the United States the population is growing faster than skilled workers in the building trades are being trained to build houses and apartments for all of these people. Every house or apartment must have a kitchen; and every kitchen must have cabinets, therefore making the cabinetmaking trade a much sought-after trade.

Since most cabinetmakers are employed by kitchen cabinet manufacturing companies, this book concentrates on the construction of kitchen cabinets and covers all phases, step by step, such as designing, drafting, millwork, cutout, assembling, laminated plastic tops, staining, finishing, and installation. The same principles used in building kitchen cabinets, however, are also used in building store fixtures, furniture, and all other types of woodworking requiring the skills of a cabinetmaker.

This book can also be used as a "Book of Standards" and a reference guide for anyone entering the cabinetmaking industry.

Chapter 11 has tables for computing all the component parts necessary to build all types and sizes of kitchen cabinets.

ACKNOWLEDGMENTS

Adjustable Clamp Company

Advanced Affiliates, Incorporated

Black and Decker Manufacturing Company

Charles Bruning Company, Incorporated

Cincinnati Tool Company

Douglas Stewart Company

Fastener Corporation

Mayline Company, Incorporated

Powermatic Houdaille

Rockwell Manufacturing Company

Stanley Power Tools

Teledyne Post Company

Wing Products Company, Incorporated

CABINETMAKING

INTRODUCTION
TO CABINETMAKING

The kitchen cabinet manufacturing companies are divided into two categories—custom cabinet manufacturers and modular cabinet manufacturers. Custom cabinets are custom built to a desired style and finish and to a required size to fit into a desired space. Modular cabinets are built in increments of 3"–24", 27", 30", 33" wide, etc. Several modular cabinets may be used to fill a required space. *Example:* If a space requiring cabinets is 93" wide, a 48" wide cabinet and a 45" wide cabinet can be used to fill the required 93" space. The same construction methods are used in building both categories of cabinets.

Both custom and modular cabinets are divided into two types: wall cabinets and base cabinets. Wall cabinets are fastened to the wall above the floor and base cabinets sit on the floor.

Both wall and base cabinets have several parts that are fabricated separately. After all parts have been fabricated, they are assembled to complete the cabinet.

1

Fig. 1   Complete kitchen.
Courtesy of Del-Mar Cabinets, Atlanta, Georgia

2

chapter 1

FABRICATION
OF THE FACEPLATE

The faceplate is the frame that is attached to the front of the cabinet. The faceplate is one of the most important parts of the cabinet because it determines the width and height of the cabinet and it is a frame on which the doors and drawers are attached. Many times it has been said that the faceplate and the doors are what really "makes" the cabinet.

There are always two parts to the faceplate, stiles (A) and rails (B). If the faceplate is wide enough, mullions (C) will be added.

Stiles (A) are the vertical pieces on each end of the faceplate. A faceplate has only two stiles: a left stile and a right stile.

Rails (B) are the horizontal pieces of the faceplate. A faceplate may have several rails.

Mullions (C) are the vertical pieces between the left and right stiles. The width of the faceplate determines how many mullions to add.

The type of finish (stain color or natural finish) that is desired for the cabinet will determine the kind of wood that should be used to build the faceplate. If the cabinet is to be stained, the faceplate should be made from poplar lumber. Poplar lumber is a medium-hard wood that takes stain well. If the cabinet is to have a natural finish, which means that only sealer and lacquer or var-

3

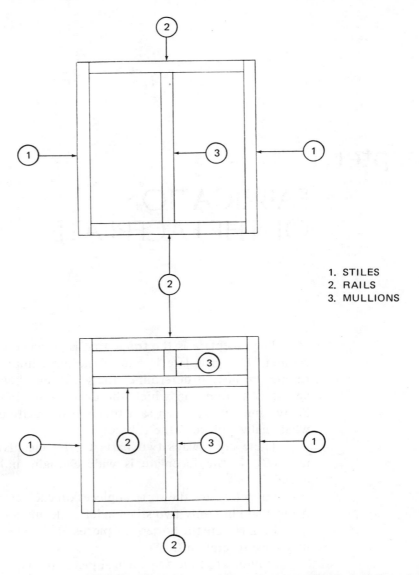

Fig. 1-1   Identifying the stiles, rails, and mulls on a wall and a base faceplate.

nish are used, the faceplate should be made from wood that matches the other exterior parts of the cabinet. *Example:* If mahogany plywood is to be used for the doors, mahogany lumber should be used for the faceplate, etc. In some instances, however, a substitute wood can be used that matches the plywood that is to be used for the doors. *Example:* If birch plywood is to be used for the doors, basswood lumber can be used instead of birch lumber for the faceplate. Basswood is softer than birch, which is an extra hard wood and much more expensive. Basswood is much easier to work with than birch and, with a natural finish, basswood looks almost identical to birch.

The lumber industry has set up standards for grading lumber. The best or select grades are called A or B grade. Many times A and B grades are combined together and sold as B and BETTER. C and D grades are not as good as A and B grades but they are much more economical and in many cases they serve the purpose just as well as A or B grade. B and BETTER grade should be used for the faceplate.

The stiles, rails, and mullions of the faceplate are cut from 3/4" thick material. Some lumber mills will sell lumber that has been planed down to any desired thickness: whereas other lumber mills only sell rough lumber. Rough lumber still has the saw marks on all four sides of the board that were made at the sawmill. Rough lumber is not graded as 1", 1-1/2", or 2" thick material; it is graded as 4/4, 6/4 or 8/4 material.

Fig. 1-2   Planer.

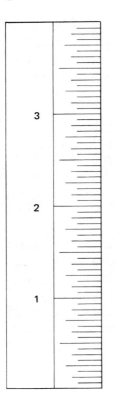

Since the faceplate parts are cut from 3/4″ thick material and if only rough lumber is available, 4/4 rough lumber and a planer must be used to obtain the required 3/4″ thick material. This 3/4″ thick material is referred to as *dressed lumber.*

Planers have a thickness guide (Fig. 1-3) that looks like a ruler. To obtain the required thickness of the lumber, first measure the thickness of the rough lumber, next set the thickness gauge on the planer at 1/16″ less than the lumber measured, and then plane off 1/16″ from each side of the lumber (moving up 1/16″ on the gauge after each cut) until the lumber has been planed down to the required thickness. *Example:* If the rough lumber measures 1″ thick, set the thickness gauge at 15/16″, then 7/8″, then 13/16″, and finally 3/4″.

Safety Rules for the Planer

1. Do not stand behind the planer while a board (thin piece of lumber) is being run through the planer; stand off to the side.
2. Do not look into the planer while it is running. A chip of wood could fly back causing serious injury.
3. Do not put hands inside the planer while it is running.
4. Do not run a board (thin piece of lumber) less than 24″ long through the planer.
5. Do not turn off the planer while a board is being run through the planer.

Fig. 1-3 Planer gauge (scale).

Fig. 1-4 Running a board through the planer.

After the rough lumber has been planed down to 3/4″ thick, one edge of each board must be run across the jointer to obtain a straight edge before the board can be ripped on the table saw. This step is necessary because rough lumber never has a straight edge and the planer only planes the sides.

The jointer has a gauge similar to the thickness gauge on the planer; this is called the *depth gauge.* The jointer gauge determines how much will be cut off the edge of the board. Set the depth gauge on the jointer at 1/16″ so that 1/16″ will be cut off the edge of the board each time that it is run across the jointer.

Before running the edge of the board across the jointer, determine which way the grain of the wood is running. The grain of the wood is the little lines on each side of the board that always run toward the edge of the board.

Always run the board *with* the grain and not *against* the grain when running it across the jointer. If the board is run against the grain, the edge of the board will be rough and will sometimes split.

WITH THE GRAIN ⟶

AGAINST THE GRAIN ⟶

Fig. 1-5 Two boards: one *with* the grain and the other *against* the grain.

Fig. 1-6 Jointer.

After determining which way the grain of the wood is running, place the right hand on the top edge of the board and press down toward the jointer bed; place the left hand on the side of the board and press toward the back fence and push the board across the jointer bed. Never allow the board to wobble; it causes an uneven cut on the edge of the board.

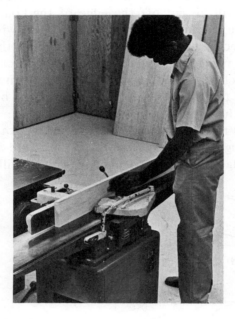

Fig. 1-7   Running a board across the jointer.

Safety Rules for the Jointer

1. Do not run a board that has a split or a loose knot in it across the jointer.
2. Keep fingers away from the knives.
3. Do not run a board less than 12″ across the jointer.

Some boards are warped sideways like the one shown in Fig. 1-8. With such a board, always run the bottom edge and *not* the top edge across the jointer.

Fig. 1-8   Board that is warped sideways.

If the arc on the bottom edge of the board is too much, rather than run the board across the jointer so many times to obtain a straight edge, use another board with a straight edge to draw a straight line across the bottom edge of the board; then cut along the straight line on the band saw. Since this is a freehand cut on the band saw, the edge won't be exactly straight but it will be straight enough so that about two more cuts across the jointer will make it straight.

Fig. 1-9 Drawing a straight line using a straightedge across a warped board.

Fig. 1-10 Cutting along the line on a band saw.

Safety Rules for the Band Saw

1. Do not adjust the saw guide while the machine is running.
2. Do not raise or lower the guide wheels while the machine is running.
3. Do not expose any more of the saw blade than is necessary.
4. Keep hands away from the saw blade while the machine is running.

After the lumber has been planed down to 3/4" thick on the planer and the edge of each board has been run across the jointer to make it straight, the next step is to rip up the boards on the table saw to the required width for the stiles, rails, and mullions. The most common width is 2". Boards that are less than 6" wide are called *strips.*

Never rip a board the exact width that is required because the saw blade on a table saw always leaves a rough edge on the board that has been cut. Always rip the board 1/8" over the required width. *Example:* Since the faceplate parts are going to be 2" wide, rip up the boards on the table saw into 2-1/8" strips; then run each edge across the jointer to cut off 1/16" from each edge, leaving each edge smooth and at the same time leaving each strip the required width of 2".

Every other tooth of a table saw blade will be set toward the fence on the table saw and every other tooth will be set away from the fence.

If the required width of a strip to be cut is 2-1/8" wide, the exact measurement from the fence to one of the saw teeth that sets toward the fence must be exactly 2-1/8".

The height of the saw blade should be set so that the blade will not rise over 1/4" above the board to be cut.

When ripping strips that are 3" wide or less, always use a push stick and not the hand to push the strip past the saw blade. *Caution:* When cutting a board on a table saw, always push the board past

Fig. 1-11 Using tape measure to set the table saw fence 2-1/8" from the saw blade.

Fig. 1-12   Using a push stick to rip a 2-1/8″ × 18″ × 3/4″ strip from a 4-1/2″ × 18″ × 3/4″ board.

the saw blade after it has been cut. Never leave the board between the blade and the fence because the board could kick back and injure the operator.

Safety Rules for the Table Saw, or Ripsaw

1. Do not let more than 1/4″ of the saw blade extend above the material that is to be cut.
2. Always push the material past the saw blade after it has been cut.
3. Use a push stick when ripping strips that are less than 3″ wide.

Now that the 3/4″ thick boards have been ripped to 2-1/8″ wide and the edges have been run across the jointer leaving the strips the required 2″ width, the faceplate parts are ready to be cut to the required length.

All boards that are 12″ wide or less should be cut to length with a radial-arm saw or, as it is sometimes called, a cutoff saw.

Before cutting a board to length, cut off one end of the board so that the end will be square and will also have a smooth cut.

Using a tape measure, measure from the square, cutoff end from left to right over to the desired length. Keep the tape measure parallel to the top edge of the board to be cut and then make a fine pencil mark on the board at the required length.

Fig. 1-13   Using the tape measure to measure parallel with the top edge of the 2-1/8″ × 18″ × 3/4″ board and make a small pencil mark 15″ from the left end.

To cut a board to the exact length required, place it where the saw blade will cut on the right side of the pencil mark. It is very important that the board be cut off on the right-hand side of the pencil mark and not through the pencil mark so that the board will be the exact length required.

Fig. 1-14   Radial-arm saw blade on the right-hand side of the pencil mark that is 15″ from the left end.

Fig. 1-15   Cutting off a board on the radial-arm saw with the left-hand holding down the board.

Place the left hand on the board to be cut off and then push the board back against the backstop. Use the right hand to pull the saw blade across the board.

If several boards are to be cut to the same length, fasten a wood clamp on the backstop of the saw at the required length and then each board can be placed against the wood clamp; this will eliminate measuring each board separately.

Fig. 1-16 Wood clamp on the fence of a radial-arm saw for "guide" or "stop" to cut several pieces of wood the same length.

Safety Rules for the Radial-Arm Saw or Cutoff Saw

1. Always hold the material that is to be cut firmly against the back fence.
2. Hold the material with the left hand and on the left-hand side of the saw blade.
3. Do not cut more than one piece of lumber at a time.
4. Keep the hands clear of the direction in which the saw blade travels.

Most faceplates are fastened together by a mortise and tenon joint. The tenon should be 5/16″ thick and 3/4″ long. The mortise should be 5/16″ wide and 13/16″ deep.

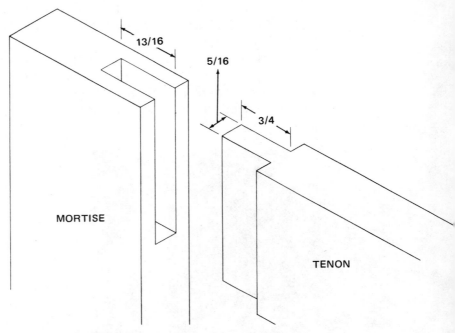

Fig. 1-17   Mortise and tenon joint.

    Stiles never have tenons, just mortises. Rails and mullions can have mortises and tenons.

    Since the tenon is 3/4″ long and is fastened inside the mortise, all faceplate parts that have a tenon on the end must have 3/4″ added to its length for each tenon.

    In Fig. 1-18, both left and right stiles are 2″ wide, 12″ long, and 3/4″ thick. The distance between the two stiles is 8″ but the rails are 9-1/2″ to allow for the 3/4″ tenon on each end.

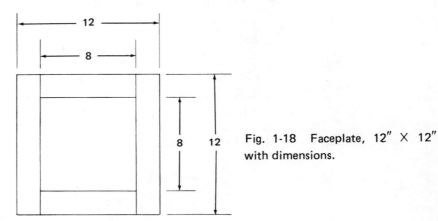

Fig. 1-18   Faceplate, 12″ × 12″ with dimensions.

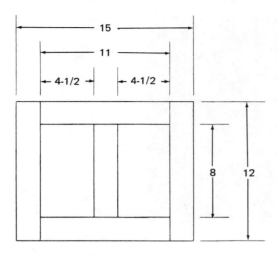

Fig. 1-19 Faceplate, 15″ × 12″ with dimensions.

In Fig. 1-19, both left and right stiles are 2″ wide, 12″ long, and 3/4″ thick. A 2″ long and 13/16″ deep mortise must be cut in each end of both stiles. The distance between the two stiles is 11″. The two rails are 2″ wide and 12-1/2″ long, allowing 3/4″ on each end for the tenons. Both rails will have a 2″ long and 13/16″ deep mortise in the center. The distance between the top and bottom rails is 8″. The mull is 2″ wide and 9-1/2″ long, allowing 3/4″ on each end for the tenons.

Before cutting the tenons on each end of the two rails and the mull, mark an "X" with a pencil on the face side (best side) of the two rails and the mull so that the face side or best side can be distinguished from the back side. This is very important because the tenon machine cuts about 1/32″ more from the back side than the face side. This ensures a good fit on the face side.

Fig. 1-20 Marking an "X" on the face side of a 2″ × 12-1/2″ × 3/4″ board before cutting a tenon.

Fig. 1-21   Using the tenon machine.

Always place the face or "X" side down on the *moving table* of the tenon machine; lock down and push into the tenon machine cutters.

Safety Rules for the Tenon Machine

1. Always fasten the material securely against the backstop and the moving bed of the tenon machine.
2. Always push the material, which is clamped to the moving bed, away from the operator. Never pull the material toward the operator.

If the tenon machine is not available, tenons can be cut on either a table saw or a radial-arm saw by attaching dado blades. Dado blades are a combination of two outside blades and several inside chippers that makes wide cuts.

Fig. 1-22   Using dados on a table saw to cut a tenon.

Fig. 1-23 Using dados on a radial-arm saw to cut a tenon.

Before cutting the mortise in the two stiles and mull, the hollow-chisel cutter on the mortise machine must be lined up with the tenons on the rails and mull. This can be checked by placing the face or "X" side of one of the rails or mull against the back fence of the mortise machine. Lower the hollow-chisel cutter and line it up with the tenon. This is very important to ensure a smooth fit on the face side of the faceplate.

Like the rails and mull, an "X" should be marked on the face side of the two stiles to distinguish the face side from the back side.

Place the face or "X" side against the back fence on the mortise machine; lock down and cut the mortises 2" wide and 13/16" deep on each end of the two stiles and center of each rail.

Fig. 1-24 Lining up the front end of the tenon with the mortising chisel.

Fig. 1-25 Using the mortising machine to cut a mortise on a 2" X 12" X 3/4" stile.

Safety Rules for the Mortising Machine

    1. Clamp the material against the back fence of the mortising machine.
    2. Do not put hands near the chisel while the machine is running.

    If a mortise machine is not available, a mortise can be made with a hollow chisel cutter attached to a drill press.

Fig. 1-26   Using a hollow-chisel cutter attached to a drill press for cutting a mortise.

    After all mortises and tenons are cut, apply glue to all tenons. Push the tenon on one end of the mullion into the mortise in the center of the top rail. Push the tenon on the other end of the mullion into the mortise in the center of the bottom rail. Push the tenon on the left ends of the top and bottom rails into the mortise in the left stile. Push the tenons on the right ends of the top and bottom rails into the mortise in the right stile.
    Use clamps to pull the joints up tight.
    Use a square to make sure that all corners are square.

Fig. 1-27 Putting mull tenons in mortises in top and bottom rails.

Fig. 1-28 Putting the left side of rail tenons in mortises in the left stile.

Fig. 1-30 Using pipe clamps to pull joints up tight on the 15″ × 12″ faceplate.

Fig. 1-29 Putting the right side of rail tenons in mortises in the right stile.

Fig. 1-31 Using a framing square to square up a faceplate.

Fig. 1-32 Using wire brads on the back side of the faceplate to hold joints together until the glue dries.

To avoid leaving the faceplate in the clamps while the glue dries, 5/8" wire brads can be nailed at each joint on the *back side* of the faceplate. This will hold the tenon in the mortise while the glue dries. If this procedure is followed, clamp the faceplate with the face down against the clamps so that the wire brads can be nailed from the *back side*.

The faceplate can now be removed from the clamps.

Fig. 1-33 Finished faceplate.

chapter 2

FABRICATION
OF COMPONENT PARTS

Ends, Shelves, Nailing Strips, Corner Blocks, Toeboards, and Backs

There are many component parts that are required to build a cabinet. Each one of these should be fabricated before attempting to assemble the cabinet.

Many of the component parts of a cabinet are made from plywood. Pound for pound, plywood is stronger than steel because it consists of several layers of thin wood glued together with the grain of every other layer running alternately. Plywood is graded very similarly to lumber. The following chart will explain the different grades of plywood.

The location of the plywood should determine the grade of the plywood to be used.

Wall Cabinet Ends

The wall cabinet ends are attached to the stiles of the faceplate. The shelves and the back are attached to these ends.

The location of the cabinet will determine the type of material that should be used for the wall cabinet ends. *Example:* If the

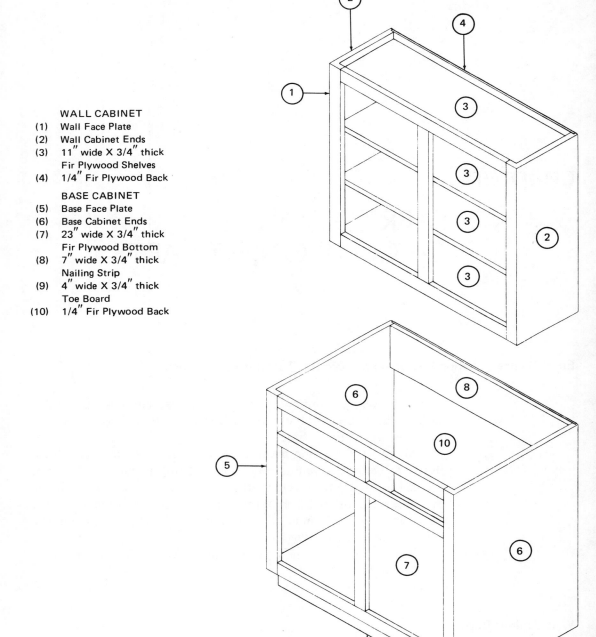

WALL CABINET
(1)   Wall Face Plate
(2)   Wall Cabinet Ends
(3)   11″ wide X 3/4″ thick
     Fir Plywood Shelves
(4)   1/4″ Fir Plywood Back

BASE CABINET
(5)   Base Face Plate
(6)   Base Cabinet Ends
(7)   23″ wide X 3/4″ thick
     Fir Plywood Bottom
(8)   7″ wide X 3/4″ thick
     Nailing Strip
(9)   4″ wide X 3/4″ thick
     Toe Board
(10) 1/4″ Fir Plywood Back

Fig. 2-1   Identifying all the component parts on a wall and base cabinet.

22

Table 2-1   Chart for grading plywood

Use these symbols when you specify plywood	Description and Most Common Uses	Veneer Grade			Most Common Thickness (Inch)					
		Face	Back	Inner Plys						
A-A	For interior applications where both sides will be on view. Built-ins, cabinets, furniture and partitions. Face is smooth and suitable for painting.	A	A	D	1/4	3/8	1/2	5/8	3/4	
A-B	For uses similar to Interior A-A but where the appearance of one side is less important and two smooth solid surfaces are necessary.	A	B	D	1/4	3/8	1/2	5/8	3/4	
A-D	For interior uses where the appearance of only one side is important. Paneling, built-ins, shelving, partitions.	A	D	D	1/4	3/8	1/2	5/8	3/4	
B-B	Interior utility panel used where two smooth sides are desired. Permits circular plugs. Paintable.	B	B	D	1/4	3/8	1/2	5/8	3/4	
B-D	Interior utility panel for use where one smooth side is required. Good for backing, sides of built-ins.	B	D	D	1/4	3/8	1/2	5/8	3/4	

wall cabinet end (left or right) butts into another cabinet or a wall, 3/4" thick B–D grade fir plywood should be used for that end. This end is usually referred to as a *blind* end. If either end (left or right) of the cabinet is exposed, which means that it will be seen from the outside of the cabinet, the same type of material that is to be used for the doors should also be used for that end. *Example:* If the doors are to be made from birch plywood, the exposed end of the cabinet should also be built from birch plywood. This end is usually referred to as a *finished* end.

The length of the wall cabinet ends are always the same as the height of the faceplate. The width of the wall cabinet ends are determined by the method in which the ends are attached to the faceplate.

There are several ways to attach the wall ends to the faceplate but the most common are the lock joint, the dado and lip joint, and the butt joint. If the lock joint is used, the wall cabinet ends are 11-15/16" wide. If the dado and lip joint is used, the wall cabinet ends are 11-1/2" wide. If the butt joint is used, the wall cabinet ends are 11-1/4" wide. The total depth of the wall cabinet, which includes the thickness of the faceplate and the width of the wall cabinet ends, must be 12", regardless of the method in which the wall cabinet ends are attached to the faceplate.

12

Fig. 2-2 Ends attached to the wall cabinet faceplate, with dimensions.

Regardless of whether the lock joint, the dado and lip joint, or the butt joint is used to attach the wall cabinet ends to the faceplate, the dados for the shelves and the rabbets for the back are all cut the same way and they should be cut before the front edges of the ends are shaped for the lock joint, the dado and lip joint, or the butt joint.

The 30" high wall cabinet should have four shelves; top, bottom, and two equally spaced center shelves. The 24" high wall cabinet should have three shelves: top, bottom, and one center shelf. The 18", 15", and 12" high wall cabinets should only have top and bottom shelves.

Dados should be cut in the wall cabinet ends where the shelves are to be located and attached. The dado cut should be 3/8″ deep and the same width as the thickness of the shelves that are to be used. If the wall cabinet end is a blind end and B–D grade fir plywood is to be used, the dados for the shelves should be cut on the good or B side of the plywood because that side should be on the inside of the cabinet and can be seen. The knotty or D side of the plywood should be on the outside of the cabinet, which cannot be seen when it butts into another cabinet or a wall.

The top and bottom shelves should be recessed slightly above and below the top and bottom rails of the faceplate. Since the width of the top and bottom rails are 2″, the far side of the dado cut should be 1-15/16″ from the top and bottom edge of the wall end so that the top and bottom shelf would recess 1/16″ above and below the top and bottom rail. The dados for the ends of a 30″ high wall cabinet should be cut as illustrated in Fig. 2-3.

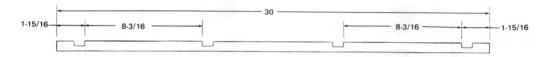

Fig. 2-3   Dados in a 30″ high wall cabinet with dimensions.

Regardless of the height of the wall cabinet, the dados for the top and bottom shelves on all wall ends should be cut 1-15/16″ from the top and bottom edge of the wall end to the far side of the dado blades.

A rabbet is a slot that is cut out of the edge of a piece of material so that another piece of material can fit into the slot.

A 1/4″ deep and 1/2″ wide rabbet should be cut on the back edges of the wall cabinet ends so that the back of the cabinet can fit into this rabbet.

There are several ways to cut rabbets, but one of the fastest is with the dado blades and the table saw.

To cut a rabbet that is less than 3/4″ deep and 3/4″ wide, it

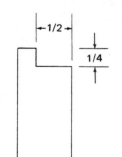

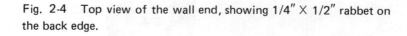

Fig. 2-4   Top view of the wall end, showing 1/4″ × 1/2″ rabbet on the back edge.

is best to clamp a piece of wood that is the same width and length as the fence to the table saw fence. Lower the dado blades below the table saw surface and move the fence over toward the dado blades where the wood that is clamped to the fence will be directly above the dado blades. Turn on the saw and gradually raise the dado blades up into the piece of wood that is clamped to the fence. *Caution:* Make sure that the dado blades will not hit the metal fence when the dado blades are being raised up into the piece of wood that is clamped to the fence.

Since the rabbet that is to be cut on the back edge of the wall cabinet ends is 1/4" deep and 1/2" wide, raise the dado blades 1/2" above the table saw surface. Move the fence over to where only 1/4" of the dado blades extend out past the edge of the piece of wood that is clamped to the fence. Test the cut for accuracy on a piece of scrap wood.

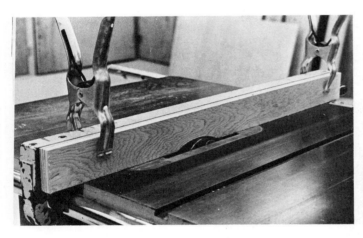

Fig. 2-5 Spring clamps holding fir plywood on a table saw fence over dado blades for cutting a 1/4" X 1/2" rabbet.

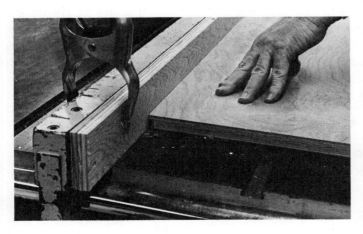

Fig. 2-6 Cutting rabbets on the back edge of 11-15/16" X 30" X 3/4" birch plywood wall end.

With the face side or outside of the wall cabinet end up, run the back edge of the wall end across the dado blades.

After the dados for the shelves and the rabbets for the back have been cut, the front edges of the wall cabinet ends are ready to be shaped for the type of joint that is to be used to attach the ends to the faceplate.

The best method for attaching the ends to the faceplate is the lock joint. The lock joint wedges together so tightly that it does not require any nails or clamps to hold it in place until the glue dries. After the joint has been sanded, it makes an almost invisible joint.

When using the lock joint on a 30" high wall cabinet faceplate, the size of the wall cabinet end is 11-15/16" wide and 30" long.

The first step in making a lock joint is to set the jointer to make a 1/16" cut and tilt back the fence at 2-1/2 degrees. Place the back or dado side of the 11-15/16" wide and 30" long wall end against the fence of the jointer and run the front edge of the wall end across the jointer two times. This will leave a 2-1/2 degree bevel on the front edge of the wall end.

Put the lock-joint cutters on the shaper and test the lock-joint cut on two pieces of 3/4" thick scrap wood. When the lock joint will wedge together and not fall apart, it is adjusted correctly.

Fig. 2-7   Running the front edge of the 11-15/16" × 30" × 3/4" wall end across the jointer with the fence tilted over 2-1/2 degrees for making a lock joint.

Fig. 2-8   End view of a lock joint.

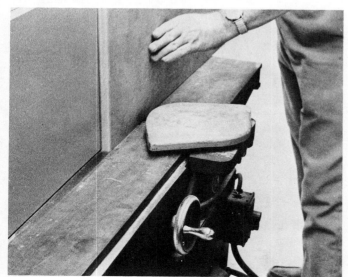

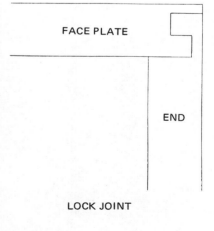

FACE PLATE

END

LOCK JOINT

After the lock-joint cutters have been set to make the right cut, place the back or dado side of the wall end against the fence of the shaper and run the front edge or bevel edge of the wall end one time across the shaper with the lock-joint cutters.

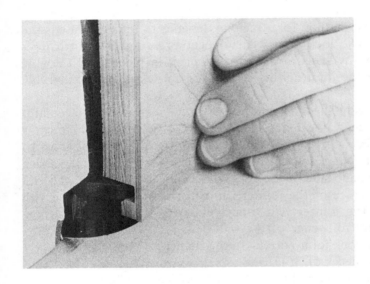

Fig. 2-9 Running the 2-1/2 degree beveled front edge of the 11-15/16″ X 30-3/4″ wall end across the shaper for making the lock joint.

After the mortises have been cut in the faceplate stiles but before the faceplate has been assembled, run the outside edge of the stile (opposite end from the mortises) with the face side up across the shaper with the lock-joint cutters.

Fig. 2-10 Running a 2″ X 30″ X 3/4″ stile across the lockjoint shaper.

Assemble the faceplate before attaching the lock joint of the stile and the wall end together.

The dado and lip joint is a good way to attach the wall ends to the faceplate stiles but it does not make an almost invisible joint like the lock joint.

On a 30″ high wall cabinet using the dado and lip joint to attach the wall end to the faceplate, the wall cabinet ends is 11-1/2″ wide and 30″ long.

A 1/4″ wide and 1/4″ long lip is cut on the back side (dado side) of the front edge of the wall end. This lip is cut on the table saw with dado blades just like the rabbet on the back edge.

A 1/4″ wide and 5/16″ deep dado is cut, on the back side of the stile, 13/16″ from the edge of the stile to the far side of the dado cut. This will leave the stile extending 1/16″ past the wall end.

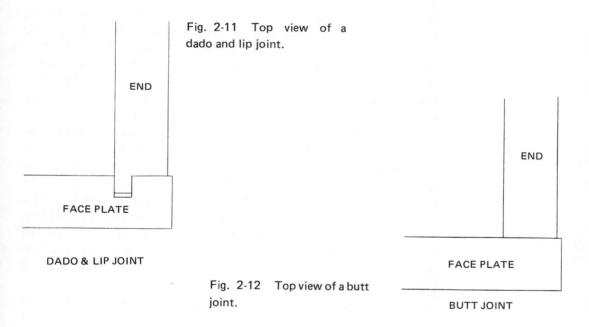

Fig. 2-11 Top view of a dado and lip joint.

END

FACE PLATE

DADO & LIP JOINT

END

FACE PLATE

BUTT JOINT

Fig. 2-12   Top view of a butt joint.

On a 30″ high wall cabinet using the butt joint to attach the wall cabinet ends to the faceplate, the wall end is 11-1/4″ wide and 30″ high.

No special cut or shape is made on the front edge of the wall end when using the butt joint. The front edge of the wall end butts into the back surface of the faceplate stile.

Base Cabinet Ends

Unlike the wall cabinet, the height of the base cabinet does not vary. The standard height of the base cabinet is 34-1/2". Like the wall cabinet, the location of the base cabinets will determine the type of material that should be used for the base cabinet ends. B–D grade 3/4" thick fir plywood is used for the blind ends and the same type of material that is to be used for the doors should also be used for the finished ends.

Like the wall cabinet, the width of the base cabinet ends are determined by the method in which the ends are attached to the faceplate. The same methods that were used to make the lock joint, the dado and lip joint, and the butt joint for attaching the wall cabinet ends to the faceplate are also used to attach the base ends to the faceplate. If the lock joint is used, the base cabinet ends are 23-15/16" wide. If the dado and lip joint is used, the base cabinet ends are 23-1/2" wide. If the butt joint is used, the base cabinet ends are 23-1/4" wide. The total depth of the base cabinet, which includes the thickness of the faceplate and the width of the base cabinet ends, must be 24", regardless of the method in which the base cabinet ends are attached to the faceplate.

The same 1/4" deep and 1/2" wide rabbet that was cut on the back edge of the wall cabinet ends are also cut on the back edge of the base cabinet ends. The same methods that were used to cut the dados in the wall cabinet ends are also used to cut the dado in the base cabinet ends although there is only one dado cut in a base cabinet end and that is for the bottom of the cabinet. This dado is cut 5-15/16" from the bottom of the base end of the far side of the dado. Like the wall cabinet blind ends, the dado for the base cabinet blind ends should also be cut on the good side or the B side of the fir plywood.

Base cabinets have toeboards that are 4" high and recessed back 2" from the front surface of the faceplate. The type of joint

Fig. 2-13 Showing the dado on the bottom of a base end.

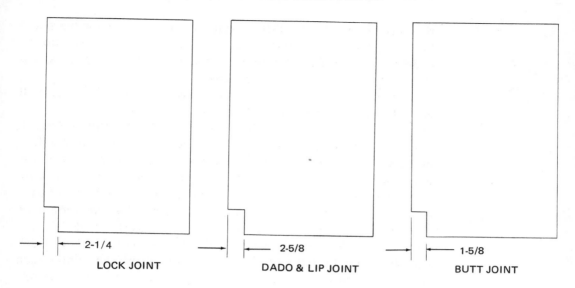

| ├── 2-1/4 | ├── 2-5/8 | ├── 1-5/8 |
| LOCK JOINT | DADO & LIP JOINT | BUTT JOINT |

Fig. 2-14 Dimensions for the toeboard cutouts for the lock joint, the dado and lip joint, and the butt joint on the base end.

used, the lock joint, the dado and lip joint, or the butt joint, also determines the amount to cut out for the toeboard on the base ends (see Fig. 2-14).

When each of the base ends in Fig. 2-14 is attached to the faceplates and the toeboards are attached to each of the toeboard cutouts in each of the base ends, the distance from the toeboard to the front surface of the faceplate will be 2".

Wall Cabinet Shelves

Since the thickness of the faceplate parts is 3/4" and if a 1/4" thick back is used, the width of the wall cabinet shelves is 11". The thickness of the faceplate and the thickness of the back plus the width of the shelves should all add up to 12", which is the standard depth of a wall cabinet.

One of the easiest and fastest ways to make a wall cabinet shelf is from 3/4" thick pine shelving. The only work that is required is to shape the front edge (flat or round), cut to length, and rip to the required 11″ width. Even though pine shelving has many knots in it and sometimes warps across the width of the board, which makes it difficult to insert in the dados in the wall ends, it is still used for shelves in many expensive cabinets.

One of the best ways to make shelves is from 3/4″ thick B–B grade fir plywood that is good on both sides.

The top and bottom shelf can be cut to the required width (11″) and length and used as it is without any other preparation because the top and bottom rails of the faceplate will cover up the edges of the plywood so that the layers of wood cannot be seen.

The center shelves should have a cap glued to the front edge so that the layers of wood cannot be seen. This cap should be 1/4″ thick and 7/8″ wide and the same length as the shelf.

Use a wide board that is 7/8″ thick to cut the 1/4″ thick caps but run the edge of the wide board across the jointer each time before cutting the 1/4″ thick cap. This will always leave one smooth surface on the cap.

Glue the smooth edge of the cap to the front edge of the fir plywood shelf with contact cement. Sand the edges of the 7/8″ wide cap that protrudes above and below the 3/4″ thick fir plywood shelf so that they are flush with the top and bottom surface of the shelf.

After the cap has been glued to the front edge of the shelf and the edges of the cap have been sanded flush with the top and bottom surface of the shelf, run the front edge (cap edge) of the shelf across the jointer to dress up the edge.

Since the 1/4″ thick cap was glued to the edge of the 11″ wide shelf, the shelf is now more than 11″ wide. Place the front edge or cap edge of the shelf against the fence of the table saw and rip the shelf back to 11″ wide.

Base Cabinet Shelves

The width of a base cabinet bottom is 23″ if the faceplate parts are 3/4″ thick and the back is 1/4″ thick. The thickness of the faceplate and the thickness of the back plus the width of the bottom should all add up to 24″, which is the standard depth of a base cabinet.

A base cabinet bottom should be made from 3/4″ thick B–D grade fir plywood. No cap is required on the front edge of the bottom because the edge will be covered by the bottom rail of the faceplate.

If a center shelf is used in a base cabinet, it should be 11″ wide and 10″ up from the bottom of the cabinet. Dados are not cut in the base ends for center shelves; the shelves are fastened to the base ends with 3/4″ thick cleats like the one in Fig. 2-15. If the center shelf is over 48″ long, a brace like the one in Fig. 2-16 should be used for support.

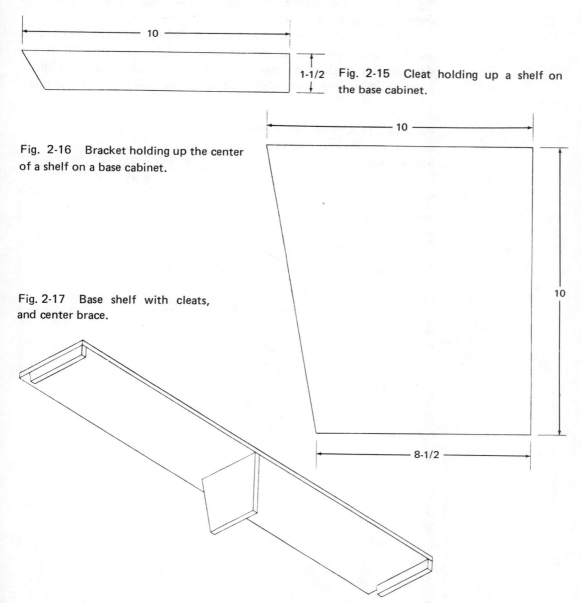

Fig. 2-15 Cleat holding up a shelf on the base cabinet.

Fig. 2-16 Bracket holding up the center of a shelf on a base cabinet.

Fig. 2-17 Base shelf with cleats, and center brace.

Nailing Strips

A nailing strip is a strip of wood that is attached to the back side of a cabinet to give the back more support so that the cabinet can be fastened to the wall.

If 1/4″ thick plywood is used for a wall cabinet back, a nailing strip is not necessary because the 1/4″ thick plywood back is strong enough to support the cabinet on the wall.

A nailing strip must be used on all base cabinets because it serves three purposes. In addition to being a nailing strip, it is a strip on which the top edge of the cabinet back is attached and it is a spacer between the top back edges of the two base cabinet ends.

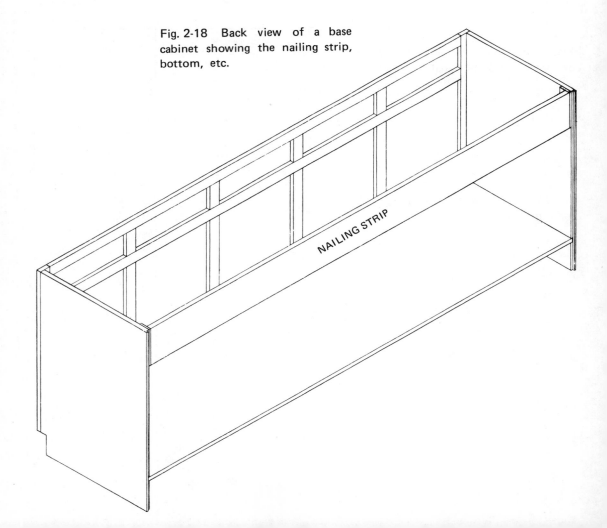

Fig. 2-18 Back view of a base cabinet showing the nailing strip, bottom, etc.

NAILING STRIP

A nailing strip should be 7″ wide and 3/4″ thick and should have a 2″ wide by 7″ long by 1/4″ thick piece of plywood attached to each end of the nailing strip. (Fig. 2-19) for attaching the nailing strips to the inside of the base cabinet ends.

The *A* dimension in Fig. 2-19 must be the same as the distance between the two base ends that are fastened to the faceplate.

The A dimension in Fig. 2-19 is the same as the B dimension in Fig. 2-20.

The nailing strip is 1/2″ less than the *B* dimension in Fig. 2-20. With the 1/4″ thick by 2″ wide by 7″ long plywood that is attached to each end of the nailing strip, the total length of the nailing strip will be the same as the *B* dimension in Fig. 2-20.

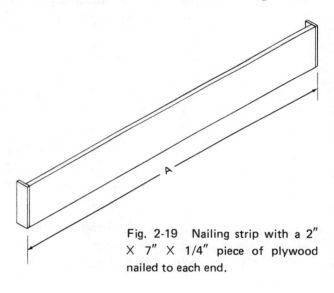

Fig. 2-19   Nailing strip with a 2″ X 7″ X 1/4″ piece of plywood nailed to each end.

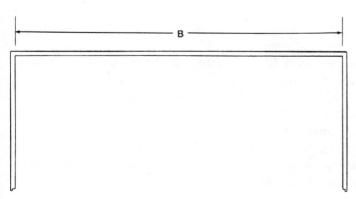

Fig. 2-20   Top view of a base cabinet, showing the faceplate, ends, and the back, with dimensions.

Corner Blocks

Corner blocks are attached to the top four corners of base cabinets for squaring up the base cabinet and for attaching the plastic top to the base cabinet.

Corner blocks should be cut from 5" X 5" X 3/4" thick wood. The best way to cut a 5" X 5" square piece of wood is to set the fence of the table saw 5" from the blade and cut the piece of wood in both directions, across and with the grain. This will make a perfect 5" X 5" square. After the 5" X 5" square piece of wood has been cut, draw a line from one corner of the block to the opposite corner (see Fig. 2-21).

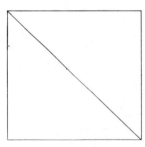

Fig. 2-21 Five by five corner blocks with a diagonal line drawn from corner to corner.

Use the band saw to cut along the diagonal line that is drawn from one corner to the other. Each 5" X 5" X 3/4" square block will make two corners blocks.

Toeboards

Toeboards are recessed back 2" from the front surface of a base cabinet faceplate so that when a person is standing close to the cabinet, his feet will fit under the cabinet into the toe space.

Toeboards are 3/4" thick, 4" wide, and the same length as the width of the base cabinet faceplate.

A 3/8" deep dado is cut on each end of the toeboard so that the toeboard can be attached to the toeboard cutouts on the base cabinet ends (see Fig. 2-22).

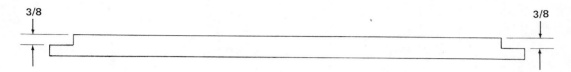

3/8   3/8

Fig. 2-22   End view of a toeboard showing a 3/8″ dado on each end.

The *A* dimension in Fig. 2-22 is the toeboard length, which is the same as the base cabinet faceplate width. The *B* dimension in Fig. 2-22 is the same as the thickness of the base cabinet ends.

Wall Cabinet Backs

Wall cabinet backs should be made from 1/4″ thick B–D grade fir plywood that is only good on one side. The back is the same width as the wall cabinet height. The length of the wall cabinet back is the same as the distance from the far side of the rabbet on one wall end to the far side of the rabbet on the other wall end. It is the same as the *A* dimension in Fig. 2-23.

Base Cabinet Backs

Base cabinet backs should be made from 1/4″ thick B–D grade fir plywood that is only good on one side. The width of the back is 23-7/8″ and the length is the same as the *A* dimension in Fig. 2-23 (same as the wall cabinet).

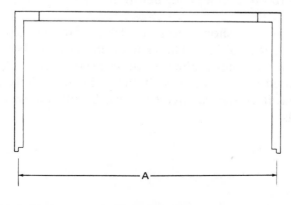

Fig. 2-23 Top view of a base cabinet showing ends and back with rabbet.

A

chapter 3

CABINET ASSEMBLY

After all the component parts of the cabinet have been fabricated, the cabinet is ready to be assembled.

The type of joint that is used to attach the ends of the cabinet to the faceplace (lock joint, dado and lip joint, or butt joint) determines the way in which the cabinet is to be assembled.

When the lock joint or the dado and lip joint is used to attach the cabinet ends to the faceplate, the cabinet ends should be attached to the faceplate before any of the other component parts of the cabinet are assembled. When the butt joint is used, the shelves are attached to the cabinet ends before the faceplate is attached to the cabinet.

Staples or nails should *never* be driven into any exposed outside surface of the cabinet. The cabinet end that butts up against the wall or into another cabinet is not an exposed end. The back is not an exposed surface because it faces the wall. Only the ends that are seen after the cabinet has been installed are exposed or finished ends.

Wall Cabinet Assembly

Lock Joint

Apply an ample amount of glue on all surfaces of the lock joint, especially the beveled edge of the wall end. Only apply glue and work on one end at a time because the glue will dry on one end while working on the other end.

Wedge the lock joint together by using clamps to pull the joint up tight. The clamps can be removed after the joint has been pulled up tight. It is not necessary to wait until the glue dries because the joint locks together (see Fig. 3-1).

Fig. 3-1 Using the twist-up clamps to pull the lock joint wall end up into the faceplate stile.

Dado and Lip Joint

Apply an ample amount of glue to the lip on the front edge of the wall cabinet end and also in the dado in the stile.

Fig. 3-2 Using the pipe clamps to pull the 11-1/2″ × 30″ × 3/4″ dado and lip joint wall end tight against the faceplate and stapling 5/8″ × 5/8″ strips to secure the wall end to the faceplate.

Use pipe clamps to pull the lip on the front edge of the wall end down into the dado in the stile. While the clamps are still holding the wall ends in place, staple or nail a 5/8″ × 5/8″ strip between each of the dados that are cut in the wall ends for the shelves. Also apply staples or nails through the 5/8″ × 5/8″ strip into the back side of the faceplate (see Fig. 3-2). This will hold the wall ends in place until the glue dries.

After the two wall ends have been attached to each end of the wall cabinet faceplate, on both the lock joint and the dado and lip joint, apply an ample amount of glue in all dados in the wall ends and to the front edges of the top and bottom shelves. Insert the shelves in the dados in the wall ends and push the shelves down until the front edges touch the back surface of the faceplate (see Fig. 3-3).

Fig. 3-3 Placing the four shelves in between the two wall cabinet ends that are attached to the faceplate.

Fig. 3-4   Using pipe clamps across the back of the cabinet to pull the wall ends up to the shelves and stapling through the rabbets to hold the wall ends to the shelves until the glue dries.

Use pipe clamps to pull the wall ends up tight against the shelf ends. Staple or nail through the rabbet surface of the wall ends into the shelves to hold the wall ends in place until the glue dries (see Fig. 3-4).

Use a pipe clamp to pull the top and bottom rail up against the edges of the top and bottom shelves. Staple or nail a 5/8″ × 5/8″ strip into the back side of the top and bottom rail and into the top and bottom shelf (see Fig. 3-5).

Fig. 3-5   Pipe clamps holding the top and bottom shelves against the faceplate and stapling 5/8″ × 5/8″ strips to the back side of the faceplate and the top and bottom shelves.

Butt Joint

When using the butt joint, the shelves are attached to the wall ends before the faceplate is attached to the cabinet.

Apply an ample amount of glue in all dados in the wall ends and insert the shelves in the dados. Staple or nail the shelves to the wall ends from the front and back edges of the wall ends.

Staple or nail 5/8″ × 5/8″ strips between each shelf and flush with the front edge of each wall end and also to the front edge of the top and bottom shelf (see Fig. 3-6).

Fig. 3-6 Wall ends with all four shelves attached in place with 5/8″ × 5/8″ strips being stapled to the wall ends between each shelf.

Apply glue to the front edges of the two wall ends and also to the front edges of the shelves.

Set the faceplate in place and clamp the faceplate to the cabinet with pipe clamps.

Staple or nail through all the 5/8″ × 5/8″ strips on the front edges of the cabinet into the back side of the faceplate (see Fig. 3-7).

Since 1/4″ thick plywood that is only good on one side is used for the backs of the cabinet, the good side of the plywood should always face toward the inside of the cabinet because the back or bad side will be up against the wall and cannot be seen.

Fig. 3-7 Pipe clamps holding the faceplate down against the front edges of the shelves and the wall ends for the butt joint.

Before attaching the back to the cabinet, place the back on the back side of the cabinet and make a pencil mark, on the back side of the back, at the center of each shelf. Do the same on each end. Use a straightedge and draw a straight line from mark to mark. This line will serve as a guide when stapleing or nailing the back on the cabinet (see Fig. 3-8).

Apply glue to the back edges of the two wall ends and to the back edges of the shelf. Set the back of the cabinet in place and staple or nail along the lines on the back of the cabinet.

Fig. 3-8 Making pencil marks on the wall cabinet back at the center of each shelf.

Wipe off all excess glue with a damp cloth. It is much easier to wipe glue off while it is still wet than to try to sand it off after it dries.

Base Cabinet Assembly

The same procedure that was used by the lock joint, the dado and lip joint, and the butt joint to attach the wall cabinet ends to the faceplate is also used to attach the base cabinet ends to the faceplate.

The same procedure that was used to attach the shelves to the wall cabinet ends and to the faceplate is also used to attach the base cabinet bottom to the base end and to the faceplate.

After the base ends have been attached to the faceplate and the bottom of the cabinet has been attached to the base ends and the faceplate, the nailing strip should be attached to the cabinet.

Apply glue to the outside surface of the 2" X 7" X 1/4" plywood that is attached to each end of the nailing strip and staple or nail through these pieces of plywood into the upper back inside surface of each of the two base ends (see Fig. 3-9).

Before the corner backs are attached to the top corners of the base cabinet, a 5/16" wide by 1-5/16" long section will have to be cut out of the two back corner blocks so that they will fit around the 2" X 7" X 1/4" piece of plywood that is attached to each end of the nailing strip.

Fig. 3-9 Attaching the nailing strip to the base cabinet by stapling through the 2" X 7" X 1/4" caps on each end of the nailing strip.

Fig. 3-10 Stapling corner blocks to the base cabinet.

Apply glue to the back edges of the corner blocks and staple or nail the front two blocks into the back sides of the base ends and faceplate. Staple or nail the back two blocks into the back side of the base ends and the nailing strip (see Fig. 3-10).

Apply glue to the edge of the cutout that was made on the bottom of each base end for the toeboard. Staple or nail each end of the toeboard to the base ends.

The toeboard is the only part of a cabinet where it is permissible to staple or nail through the exposed or outside surface. The toeboard is usually painted black and is next to the floor so the staple or nail holes will not show.

When a shelf is installed in a base cabinet, a 1-1/2″ × 10″ × 3/4″ cleat is attached to the inside of the base end where the top of the cleat will be 10″ from the bottom of the cabinet. The easiest way to attach the 1-1/2″ × 10″ × 3/4″ cleat, where it is 10″ to the top of the cleat, is to hold an 8-1/2″ long piece of lumber up next to the inside of the base end and let it rest on the base bottom, apply glue to the back surface of the cleat, and staple or nail the cleat to the inside surface of the base end.

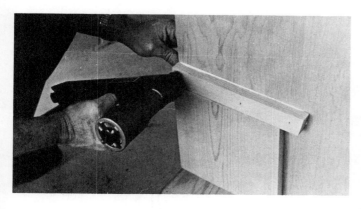

Fig. 3-11 Stapling a 1-1/2″ × 10″ × 3/4″ cleat to the base end by using an 8-1/2″ × 8-1/2″ × 3/4″ spacer to hold the 1-1/2″ × 10″ × 3/4″ cleat in place.

If the shelf that extends from one base end to the other base is over 48″ long, it should have a 10″ wide and 10″ long brace to support the shelf. If the shelf does not extend from one base end to the other base end, the same 10″ wide and 10″ long brace is attached 1-1/2″ back from the end of the shelf for support (see Fig. 3-12).

Just like the wall cabinets, the 1/4″ thick plywood that is only good on one side is also used for the backs on the base cabinet. The good side of the plywood should always face the inside of the cabinet.

Apply glue to the back edges of the base ends, the back edge of the bottom, and the nailing strip, and staple or nail the back to the cabinet.

Fig. 3-12   Attaching a 10″ × 10″ × 3/4″ shelf brace 1-1/2″ from the end of the shelf.

chapter 4

FABRICATION OF DOORS

As stated in Chapter 1, in addition to the faceplate, the doors are what really "make" the cabinet. The style of the cabinet (Early American, French Provencial, Spanish, etc.) is determined by the style of the doors.

There are so many different types and styles of doors that it would almost be impossible to mention all of them. This chapter covers four of the most popular types of doors. By using the same principles that are used to build these four different types of doors and with a little creativeness by the cabinetmaker, there is no limit to how many different styles or types of doors that can be built.

The first step in building a door is to determine what size it should be. This is done by measuring the opening (width and height) in the faceplate where the door will go and adding 5/8" to the width and height. This opening is referred to as the door opening.

Example: In Fig. 4-1, the door opening in the faceplate is 14" wide and 26" high. By adding 5/8" to the width and height of the door opening, the exact size of the door will be 14-5/8" wide and 26-5/8" high. This formula (+5/8") is used on all doors, regardless of the style, that use a 3/8" inset hinge, which is the most common hinge used on cabinet doors.

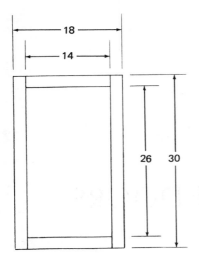

Fig. 4-1   An 18″ × 30″ wall cabinet faceplate, with dimensions.

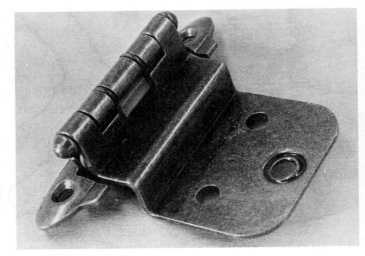

Fig. 4-2   A 3/8″ inset hinge.

The easiest and simplest door to build is the plain 3/4″ thick plywood door. By adding 5/8″ to both the width and the height of the door opening to determine the size of the door, the door is then cut from a piece of 3/4″ thick A–B grade plywood that has an outside veneer that is the same type of wood as the faceplate. *Reminder:* The width is always across the grain of the plywood and the length is always with the grain.

After the door is cut to the exact width and length, the door edges must be shaped before the door can be attached to the cabinet. This is done by using a shaper with a door-lip cutter.

The fence on the shaper, unlike the fence on the table saw and the jointer, is in two pieces: left fence and right fence. The left fence is lined up with the cutter edge, which never has to be changed once it has been set. The right fence regulates the amount to be cut off the edge of the door. The amount that is cut off the edge of the door is determined by how far the right fence is set behind the cutter edge, which should be 1/16″ on a cabinet door.

The spindle of the shaper has a shaft on which the door-lip cutter is attached. It can be moved up and down to any desired location. To shape the edges of a door, the spindle must be set where the door-lip cutter will remove just the right amount from the back side of the door so that the 3/8″ inset hinge will fit flush

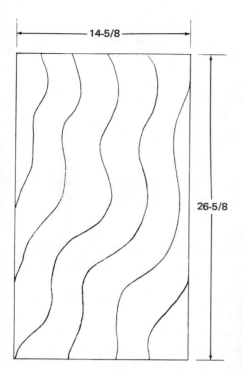

Fig. 4-3 A 14-5/8″ × 26-5/8″ × 3/4″ plain plywood door showing the grain of the wood running lengthwise.

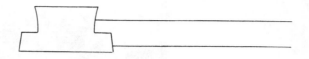

Fig. 4-4 Door-lip cutter with a door edge that has been shaped next to it.

Fig. 4-5 Shaper.

Fig. 4-6 Top view of a shaper showing fence, cutter, and door being shaped.

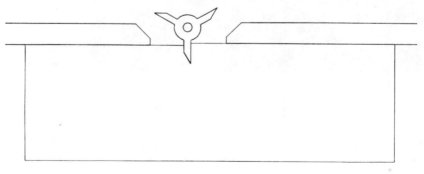

49

Fig. 4-7   Hinge in place on a piece
of scrap wood to test for fit.

with the back surface of the door and the bottom of the doorlip.
Always test the cut on a piece of scrap wood before making the
cut on the door edge.

Place the back side of the door on the shaper table; then push
the door across the door-lip cutter. The first cut should be across
the grain of the door; then rotate the door in a counterclockwise
direction to shape the other three edges of the door. This first cut
across the grain of the door sometimes splits the wood on the back
edge of the door. By rotating the door in a counterclockwise
direction, the next cut, which will be with the grain, will cut off
any part of the wood that splits.

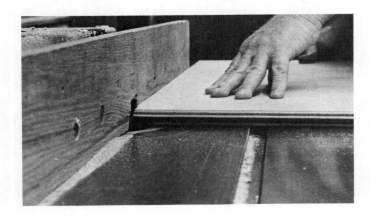

Fig. 4-8   Shaping a plain plywood
door edge on a shaper.

Safety Rules for the Shaper

1. Feed the material in the direction that is against the
   direction in which the shaper cutters are turning.

2. Never back up material. Only run in a forward motion.
3. Always keep the shaper bed clean and free from wood shavings.

This plain plywood door can be dressed up and changed into a French Provincial door by routing a French Provincial design on the face side of the door.

An adjustable provincial template, a router with a template guide, and a router bit must be used to route a French Provincial design in the door.

Place the template guide of the router against the corner of the provincial template and move the router in a clockwise direction, letting the router follow the edges of the provincial template. *Reminder:* Always start the router from a corner of the provincial template and never from the center.

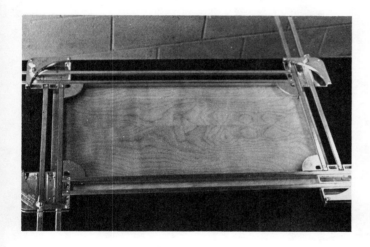

Fig. 4-9   Plain plywood door in a wing provincial template.

Fig. 4-10   Router showing a template guide and bit.

Fig. 4-11   Using a router to make a provincial route in a door.

Fig. 4-12   Door after it has been routed.

After the design has been routed in the door, the routed-out design should be painted darker than the doors and cabinets will be stained so that the design will stand out. This can be done with an artist's paintbrush.

The design should be painted before the rest of the door is stained. If any paint gets on the top surface of the door, it can easily be sanded off with the belt sander.

52

Fig. 4-13   Painting the provincial route in the door.

Fig. 4-14   Sanding off excess paint from around the route with the belt sander.

The most elegant of all cabinet doors is the raised-panel door. Even with its elegance and complicated looks, it is a simple door to build. The raised-panel door is built similarly to a one-door faceplate. It has two stiles and a top and bottom rail that are fastened together with a joint similar to the mortise and tenon joint. The raised panel is inserted between the two stiles and the top and bottom rails.

The first step in building a raised-panel door is just like the first step in building any other type of door; that is, determine the exact size of the door. The same formula of adding 5/8" to the width and height of the door opening in the faceplate is also used to determine the exact size of the raised-panel door.

Fig. 4-15   A raised-panel door.

The stiles and rails of the raised-panel door are 2-1/4″ wide and 7/8″ thick. The stiles are the same length as the door height. The rails are 3-3/4″ less than the door width. The raised panel is 3-3/4″ less than the door width and the door height and is 9/16″ thick.

In the one-door faceplate in Fig. 4-16, the door opening is 14″ wide and 26″ high. The door size is 14-5/8″ × 26-5/8″: The two stiles are 2-1/4″ wide by 26-5/8″ long by 7/8″ thick. The two rails are 2-1/4″ wide by 10-7/8″ long (width‒3-3/4″) by 7/8″ thick. The raised panel is 10-7/8″ wide (width‒3-3/4″) by 22-7/8″ (length‒3-3/4″) by 9/16″ thick.

Three separate shaper cutters are used to shape the rails, stiles, and raised panel.

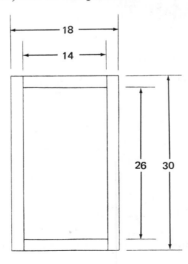

Fig. 4-16   An 18″ × 30″ wall cabinet faceplate, with dimensions.

The end cutter in Fig. 4-17 shapes the ends of the rails. The edge cutter in Fig. 4-18 shapes one edge of each rail and one edge of each stile. The panel cutter in Fig. 4-19 shapes the panel on all four edges.

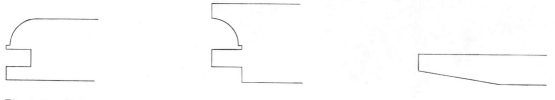

Fig. 4-17   Raised panel end cutter.

Fig. 4-18   Raised panel edge cutter.

Fig. 4-19   Raised panel panel cutter.

After all parts have been shaped, sand off the fuzz on the front edges of the stiles and rails with 220-grit sandpaper. *Do not* sand the ends of the two rails. Sand the front and back surface of the panel with the belt sander, using a 120-grit sanding belt, and then with the orbital (vibrator) sander, using 120-grit sandpaper.

The stiles, rails, and panel are assembled just like a faceplate. Apply glue to each end of the two rails and attach one end of each of the two rails to the top and bottom edge of one of the stiles. Insert the panel in place and attach the other stile to the opposite ends of the two rails and the panel edge.

Place the door in the pipe clamps with the face side down toward the clamp. Tighten the clamps and staple or nail small staples or wire brads through each end of the rails into the stiles. This will hold the door together until the glue dries. With a damp cloth, wipe off all glue that might ooze from between the joints before the glue dries.

Shape the edges of the raised-panel door on the shaper, using the door-lip cutter.

The Spanish door is built very similarly to the raised-panel door. The only difference is the width and shape of the top and bottom rails and the panel.

The stiles of the Spanish door are 2-1/4" wide and 7/8" thick but the rails are 3-1/4" wide and 7/8" thick. The panel is made from 1/4" thick A–B grade plywood with the top veneer being the same type of wood as the stiles and rails of the door.

Fig. 4-20   A Spanish door.

The length of the stiles is the same as the door height. The length of the rails is 3-3/4″ less than the door width. The 1/4″ thick plywood panel is 3-3/4″ less than the door width and the door height.

In the one-door faceplate in Fig. 4-21, the door opening is 14″ wide and 26″ high. The door size is 14-5/8″ × 26-5/8″. The two stiles are 2-1/4″ wide by 26-5/8″ long by 7/8″ thick. The two rails are 3-1/4″ wide by 10-7/8″ long (width-3-3/4″) by 7/8″ thick. The panel is 10-7/8″ wide (width – 3-3/4″) by 22-7/8″ (length-3-3/4″) by 1/4″ thick.

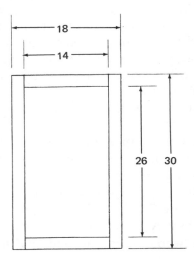

Fig. 4-21   An 18″ × 30″ wall cabi-net faceplate, with dimensions.

The end cutter in Fig. 4-17 shapes the ends of the rails. The edge cutter in Fig. 4-18 shapes one edge of each stile and the curved edge of each rail, but a special fence must be attached to the shaper before the curved edge of the rails can be shaped.

Regardless of the length of the rail (*C* dimension) in Fig. 4-22, the dimension from the edge of rail to top of the arc (*H* dimension) must always be 1″, which means that the radius (*R* dimension) will change with every different rail length.

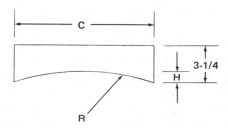

Fig. 4-22   A Spanish door rail, with dimensions.

The formula for computing the radius, according to the different lengths of the rail in Fig. 4-22, is

$$R = \frac{C^2 + 4H^2}{8H}$$

Example: For a 15″ rail,

$$R = \frac{C^2 + 4H^2}{8H}$$

$$R = \frac{(15)^2 + 4(1)^2}{8(1)}$$

$$R = \frac{225 + 4}{8}$$

$$R = \frac{229}{8}$$

$$R = 28.625$$

On a 15″ long rail (*C* dimension), the radius (*R* dimension) would be 28.625″ for the dimension from the edge of the rail to the top of the arc (*H* dimension) to be 1″.

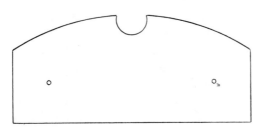

Fig. 4-23 A curved-shaper fence for shaping Spanish door rails.

To shape the edge of a rail that has an arc, a special fence that has the same arc as the rail must be attached to the shaper (see Fig. 4-23).

Example: If the rail is 15″ long (*C* dimension), the radius would be 28.625″ on both the arc on the rail and the shaper fence.

Use the shaper fence as a template to mark the arc on the rail, Fig. 4-24; then cut out the arc on the rail with the band saw.

Place the curved edge of the rail against the curved-shaper fence and run the edge of the rail across the shaper cutters in the

Fig. 4-24 Drawing the arc on a Spanish door rail using a curved fence as a template.

Fig. 4-25 Shaping a curved Spanish door rail on the shaper with the curved fence.

same manner as a straightedge running across a straight-shaper fence.

The arc on every different rail length will have a different radius and a different shaper fence. A set of shaper fences can be made from 3/4" thick plywood.

If two 2-1/2 HP (horsepower) portable routers are available, a set of templates, Fig. 4-26, can be made to route and shape the arc side of the rails with the routers. One router cuts the arc and the other router shapes the edges. The same formula that was used to make the curved-shaper fence in Fig. 4-23 is also used to determine the radius of the arcs on the router template guides.

Fig. 4-26   A Spanish door template with the template guide in place.

Fig. 4-27   Routing a curved rail on a Spanish door jig.

The 1/4″ thick plywood panel should have a 1/8″ wide by 1/8″ deep dado cut 3″ on centers on the face side of the panel.

Since most carbide saw blades are 1/8″ thick, a single blade can be used by letting only 1/8″ of the blade extend above the surface of the table saw.

There are two ways to lay out where the 1/8″ wide by 1/8″ deep dados will be cut on the 1/4″ thick plywood panel. Find the center line of the panel and make a pencil mark every 3″ in both directions. If the last pencil mark is less than 1-1/2″ from the edge of the panel, then make a pencil mark 1-1/2″ on each side of the center line of the panel and mark every 3″ in both directions from those pencil marks (see Fig. 4-28).

Place the panel on the table saw with the pencil mark (where the dado is to be cut) in the center of the saw blade and move the fence of the table saw over to the edge of the panel. Two cuts can

Fig. 4-28   Two Spanish door panels with the 1/8″ × 1/8″ dados 3″ from the center line on one door and 1-1/2″ from the center line on the other door.

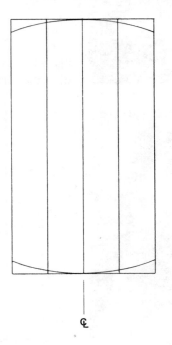

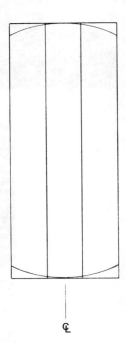

usually be made from each setup because each dado will be the same distance from each edge of the panel.

Use the band saw to cut an arc on each end of the panel so that the panel will fit into the arc on the rails.

The stiles, rails, and panels of the Spanish door are assembled just like the raised-panel door.

Shape the edges of the Spanish door on the shaper, using the door-lip cutter.

chapter 5

FABRICATION OF DRAWERS

The drawer front is the part of a drawer that is visible on the front of a cabinet when the drawer is closed. The style of the drawer fronts is determined by the style of the doors that are used on the cabinet. The dimensions of the drawer fronts are determined just like the doors, by adding 5/8" to the width and height of the drawer opening the faceplate.

The width of the drawer sides and the front and back ends of the drawer is 3/8" less than the height of the drawer opening in the faceplate. *Example:* If the drawer opening height in the face-plate is 4-1/2", the drawer sides and the front and back ends of the drawer are 4-1/8" wide.

The width of the drawer (not the drawer front) is determined by the type of drawer hardware or drawer guides that are to be used. If a monorail-type drawer guide is used, the width of the drawer is 1/4" less than the faceplate opening. If a side-mounted drawer guide is used, the width of the drawer is 1-1/16" less than the faceplate opening.

Regardless of the type of drawer guides that are used, the front and back ends and the sides of the drawers should be 1/2" thick. The length of the drawer sides should be 18" long. The drawer bottom should be 1/4" thick.

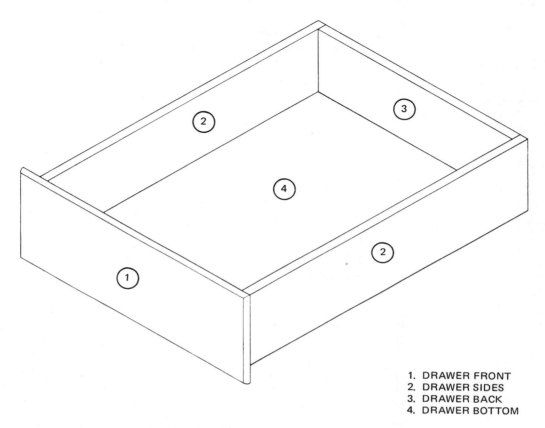

1. DRAWER FRONT
2. DRAWER SIDES
3. DRAWER BACK
4. DRAWER BOTTOM

Fig. 5-1   Identifying all parts of the drawer.

The easiest and simplest drawer to build is just like the easiest and simplest door; add 5/8″ to the width and height of the face-plate opening and cut out the drawer front from a piece of 3/4″ thick A–B grade plywood that is the same type of plywood as that used for the doors.

In Fig. 5-2, the drawer front would be 5-1/8″ wide (4-1/2″ + 5/8″) × 14-5/8″ long (14″ + 5/8″) × 3/4″ thick.

Shape the edges of the 5-1/8″ × 14-5/8″ × 3/4″ drawer front on the shaper using the door-lip cutter (just like the doors in Chapter 4).

If a monorail-type drawer guide is to be used (in Fig. 5-2), the drawer itself will be 13-3/4″ wide (14″ − 1/4″). Since the drawer sides are 1/2″ thick, the inside of the drawer will be 12-3/4″. Dado

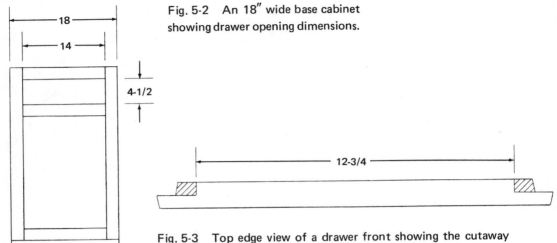

Fig. 5-2   An 18″ wide base cabinet
showing drawer opening dimensions.

18

14

4-1/2

12-3/4

Fig. 5-3   Top edge view of a drawer front showing the cutaway
for drawer sides.

off an equal amount on each end of the back side of the drawer
front so that 12-3/4″ will be left (see Fig. 5-3).

Cut a back end for the drawer that is 4-1/8″ wide (4-1/2″
− 3/8″) × 12-3/4″ long (same as the back side of the drawer front)
× 1/2″ thick. Cut two sides that are 4-1/8″ wide (4-1/2″ − 3/8″)
× 18″ long × 1/2″ thick. The bottom is 13-1/4″ × 17-3/4″ × 1/4″
plywood.

Cut a 1/4″ wide and 1/4″ deep dado, 1/4″ from the bottom
edge of the 4-1/8″ × 12-3/4″ × 1/2″ back end and the two 4-1/8″
× 18″ × 1/2″ sides (see Fig. 5-4). In the same location as on the
two sides, cut a 1/4″ wide and 3/8″ deep dado on the back side of
the drawer front. The drawer bottom will fit in these dados.

Staple or nail the two 4-1/8″ × 18″ × 1/2″ drawer sides to
the back side of the drawer front. Insert the bottom in the dados
in the drawer sides and staple or nail the back edges of the drawer
sides into the back end of the drawer (see Fig. 5-5).

The best method of construction for a drawer is a box-type
drawer. This type has a front and back end and two sides, all of
which are assembled together before the drawer front is attached.

The best method for attaching the front and back ends to the
two sides is with the dovetail joint. The dovetail is an interlocking
device for joining the corners of the drawer without the use of
staples or nails.

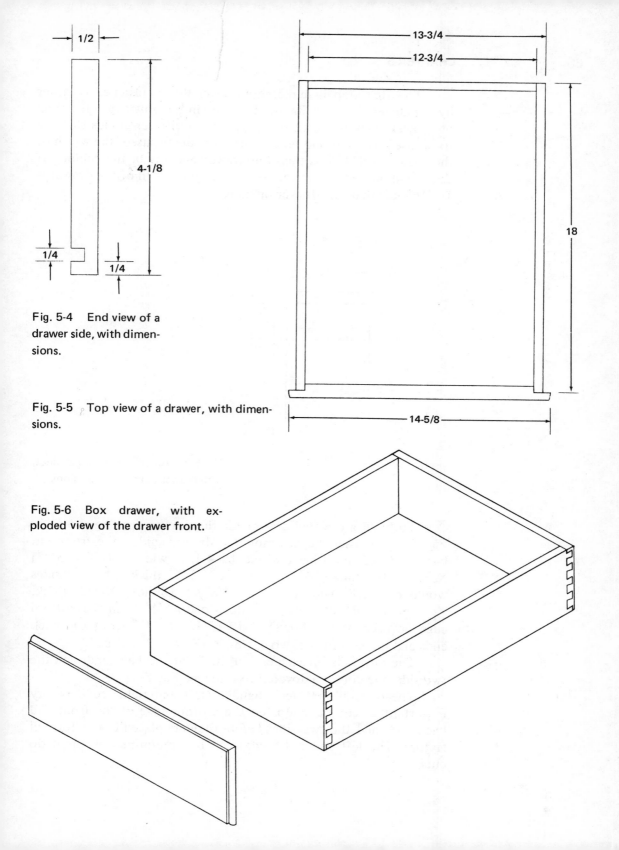

1/2

4-1/8

1/4

1/4

13-3/4

12-3/4

18

14-5/8

Fig. 5-4 End view of a drawer side, with dimensions.

Fig. 5-5 Top view of a drawer, with dimensions.

Fig. 5-6 Box drawer, with exploded view of the drawer front.

The first step in building a drawer that is fastened together by the dovetail is just like the first step in building any other type of drawer; that is, determine the type of drawer guides that are to be used. If the monorail-type drawer guide is used, the width of the drawer is 1/4″ less than the drawer opening in the cabinet. If the side-mounted drawer guide is used, the width of the drawer is 1-1/16″ less than the drawer opening.

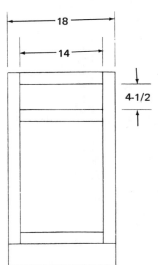

Fig. 5-7   An 18″ wide base cabinet, with drawer-opening dimensions.

To build a dovetail drawer for the drawer opening shown in Fig. 5-7 that uses the side-mounted drawer guides, the front and back ends of the drawer would be 4-1/8″ wide (4-1/2″ − 3/8″) × 12-15/16″ long (14″ − 1-1/16″) × 1/2″ thick. The two sides would be 4-1/8″ wide (4-1/2″ − 3/8″) × 18″ long × 1/2″ thick.

Cut a 1/4″ wide by 1/4″ deep dado 1/4″ from the bottom edge on each of the 4-1/8″ × 12-15/16″ × 1/2″ front and back ends and on each of the two 4-1/8″ × 18″ × 1/2″ sides.

The dovetails on each end of the front and back ends and the two sides are cut on a dovetail fixture (see Fig. 5-8).

The dovetail fixture is handed (left and right) so it is very important to cut the dados on the bottom edge of the front and back ends and the two sides *before* they are placed in the dovetail fixture. The left and right sides can be determined by the dado cuts.

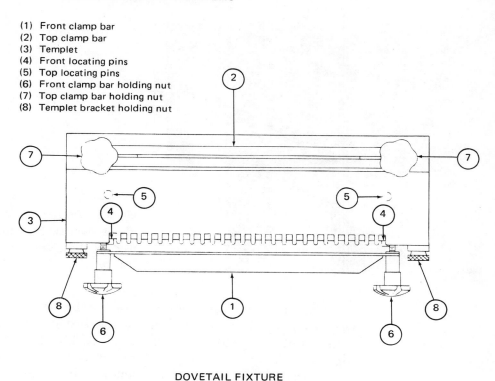

(1) Front clamp bar
(2) Top clamp bar
(3) Templet
(4) Front locating pins
(5) Top locating pins
(6) Front clamp bar holding nut
(7) Top clamp bar holding nut
(8) Templet bracket holding nut

DOVETAIL FIXTURE

Fig. 5-8   Dovetail fixture, identifying all parts.

The dovetail fixture has a locating pin on each end of the top surface and on each end of the front surface. These pins are guides for lining up the front and back ends and the sides of the drawer in their proper positions.

Always place the front and back ends of the drawer, with the dados away from the locating pin, on the top surface of the dovetail fixture. Always place the two drawer sides, with the dados away from the locating pin, on the front surface of the dovetail fixture. The clamp bar on the top and front surface of the fixture holds the drawer ends and sides in place.

Remove the finger template and fasten the drawer sides, with the dado away from the locating pin, on the front surface of the dovetail fixture with about 1/4″ of the edges extending above the top surface of the fixture (see Fig. 5-9).

Fig. 5-9   Drawer sides on the front of the dovetail jig, with 1/4″ extending above the top surface of the jig.

Place the front and back ends of the drawer, with the dado away from the locating pin, on the top surface of the dovetail fixture. Butt the ends of the front and back ends of the drawer into the back surface of the drawer sides that are fastened to the front surface of the fixture and extending about 1/4″ above the top surface of the fixture. With the ends of the front and back ends of the drawer butting into the back surface of the drawer sides, this will square up the ends of the drawer ends and sides in the dovetail fixture (see Fig. 5-10).

Fasten down the finger template with the back surface of the finger template flush against the top surface of the front and back ends. Loosen the front clamp bar that holds the drawer sides on the front surface of the dovetail fixture and butt the ends of the drawer sides into the bottom surface of the finger template (see Fig. 5-11).

A portable router with a dovetail-router bit and a template guide that fits the slots in the finger template must be used to make a dovetail cut.

The dovetail-router bit must extend below the router base exactly 19/32″. This can be measured accurately by making a fine pencil mark exactly 19/32″ from the edge of a small piece of wood. Adjust the router depth so that the bottom edge of the dovetail-router bit lines up with the pencil mark that is 19/32″ from the edge of the piece of wood (see Fig. 5-12). The dovetail

Fig. 5-10 Front and back ends attached to the top surface of the dovetail jig with the ends butting into the back surface of the sides that are attached to the front of the jig.

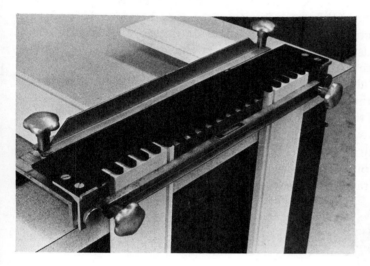

Fig. 5-11 Sides, front and back ends, and finger template all in place and ready to be routed.

Fig. 5-12 Lining up a router bit with pencil mark on a 3″ × 10″ × 3/4″ block of wood that is 19/32″ from the edge.

joint will not fit properly unless the router bit is *exactly* 19/32"
down from the router base.

Place the edge of the router base on the finger template of
the dovetail fixture before turning on the router. Let the template
guide on the router follow the slots in the finger template of the
dovetail fixture and cut from left to right.

Caution: Since the dovetail-router bit flares out at the bottom,
never lower the router or lift the router from the finger template
because the router bit will cut into the finger template. After the
dovetails have been cut, turn the router off before removing it
from the dovetail fixture.

Since the dovetail fixture is handed (left and right), the ends
of the front and back ends and the sides of the drawer are also
handed. If the ends of the front and back ends or the sides of the
drawer are cut on the left-hand side of the dovetail fixture, the
opposite ends will have to be cut on the right-hand side of the
dovetail fixture. If the front and back ends and the sides of the
drawer are always placed in the dovetail fixture with the dado
away from the locating pin, it is easy to determine which end has
to be cut on the left or right side of the dovetail fixture.

The drawer bottom width is 1/2" less than the front and back
ends of the drawer. If 18" drawer sides are used, the drawer bottom
is 17-5/8" long. The drawer bottom should be made from 1/4"
thick A–D grade fir plywood.

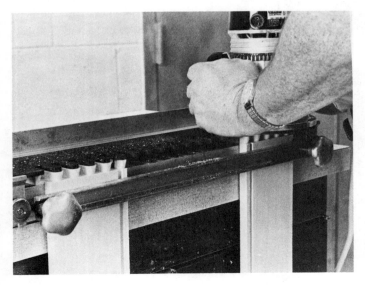

Fig. 5-13 Cutting dovetails on a
jig.

The drawer bottom in Fig. 5-7 is 12-7/16″ wide (12-15/16″ − 1/2″) × 17-5/8″ long × 1/4″ thick.

Apply glue on all dovetail cuts, insert the bottom in the dados, and tap the drawer sides down with a rubber hammer into the dovetail cutouts in the front and back ends of the drawer. It is not necessary to staple or nail the drawer ends to the drawer sides because the dovetail joint will hold together until the glue dries.

After the glue has dried and the drawer has been sanded, the drawer front can be attached to the front edge of the drawer by stapling or nailing through the front edge of the drawer into the back surface of the drawer front.

If raised-panel doors are used on the cabinet, the drawer front should be shaped like the one in Fig. 5-14.

If Spanish doors are used on the cabinet, the drawer front should be shaped like the one in Fig. 5-15.

Fig. 5-14   End view of a raised-panel drawer front.

Fig. 5-15   End view of a Spanish drawer front.

chapter 6

SANDING, STAINING, AND FINISHING

The prerequisite of a good finish on a cabinet is a careful sanding job. Stain will not cover up cracks or scratches on the cabinet; if anything, it tends to make them show up more.

Even though a cabinet might be built as perfectly as possible, there are still small cracks anywhere two pieces of wood are joined together. First fill up all of these cracks with wood dough before sanding. Wood dough is a putty-like substance that looks and feels like real wood after it dries.

Wood dough shrinks as it dries. A putty knife should not be used to apply wood dough because if the excess is scraped off from around the crack, another crack will be formed as the wood dough dries.

Wood dough should be applied with the fingers and an ample amount should be left piled above the crack so that when the wood dough dries, a small portion will still be piled above the crack. *Important:* Never sand wood dough while it is wet. Not only does it gum up the sandpaper, it will also continue to shrink as it dries and still leave a crack.

Even though wood dough dries on the top surface rather quickly, it may still be wet underneath. Apply it at the end of the workday and allow it to dry overnight. This gives the wood dough a chance to set firmly, which makes it much easier to sand.

The ideal way to sand faceplates and doors is with a three-drum sander. A three-drum sander looks very similar to a planer. Instead of having cutter knives like the planer, it has three drums with course, medium, and fine sandpaper attached to them that does the complete sanding job with one pass through the machine. The three-drum sander is sometimes too expensive for the smaller cabinet shops, however, and the sanding has to be done with a portable belt sander and an orbital or vibrator sander.

Important: The first rule to remember in sanding is *never* to sand across the grain of the wood. This prevents scratches on the wood that are almost impossible to sand out.

Use 120-grit sandpaper on the portable belt sander and sand off all wood dough and high spots (faceplate joints, etc.) on the cabinet. Never hold the belt sander in one place to sand; always keep it moving. This will eliminate sanding too deeply in the wood.

Since most faceplate parts are 2″ wide, it is difficult to keep from sanding across the grain on some of the faceplate parts. With a little caution, however, this can be reduced to a minimum.

Sand in the sequence and in the direction of the arrows that are shown in Fig. 6-1. Even though there might be sanding scratches across the grain on some of the faceplate parts, these scratches can be sanded off when sanding in the next sequence and in the direction in which the arrow is pointing.

The stiles and rails of the raised-panel and Spanish doors should be sanded (front and back) in the same sequence and in the same direction as shown in Fig. 6-2, which is basically the same procedure as that used for the faceplates.

After the cabinet and doors have been sanded with the belt sander, use 120-grit sandpaper on the orbital or vibrator sander and sand over the entire cabinet and doors.

The orbital or vibrator sander will sand out any scratches that were made by the belt sander.

Important: Never use worn sandpaper on the orbital or vibrator sander because it tends to polish the wood rather than to sand it. Even though the polished wood looks and feels smooth, stain cannot penetrate it. The stain just stands and dries on top of the wood.

Use the air hose to blow the sawdust from the cabinet and inspect the cabinet very closely for any small scratches that might have been overlooked. Small scratches are sometimes hard to see on the natural wood but they really stand out after the cabinet has been stained.

After the cabinet has been completely sanded, use 220-grit

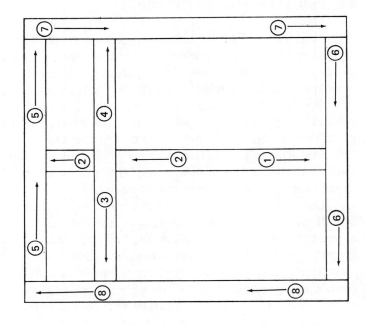

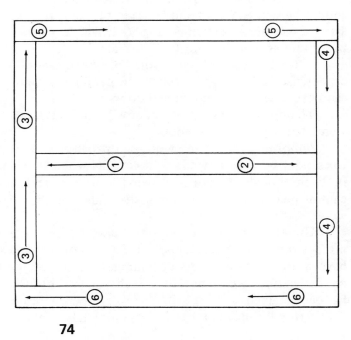

Fig. 6-1 A wall and a base cabinet faceplate, with arrows showing sanding directions.

74

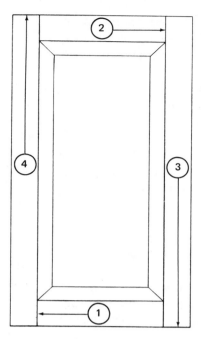

Fig. 6-2   Raised-panel door, with arrows for sanding directions.

sandpaper and sand off (by hand) the fuzz on all edges. Slightly round off the edges on each end of the faceplate.

There are so many different types of stain and ways to stain a cabinet that it would almost be impossible to mention all of them. Basically there are two kinds of stain: a spray-on stain and a rub-on stain. Usually a rub-on stain cannot be sprayed on and a spray-on stain cannot be rubbed on.

One of the best ways to finish a cabinet is with a spray. A spray-on finish will always look better than a hand-brushed finish.

The difference between stain and paint is that stain, no matter how dark it is, will always show the grain of the wood.

There is an old theory that if a darker cabinet is desired, more stain is applied until it turns dark. This theory is wrong. If a darker cabinet is desired, use a darker stain. If a lighter cabinet is desired, use a lighter stain. Never try to spray a light coat of dark stain to obtain a light cabinet or to spray several coats of light stain to obtain a darker cabinet. Several coats of most stains will practically cover the grain of the wood. It makes the cabinet look as if it had been painted rather than stained.

There are many different kinds of spray guns and spray equipment. Some spray guns have a cup attached that holds about a quart of paint; while other spray guns are connected to a spray tank that holds several gallons of paint. Both types do an adequate job. Note that the spray cup and spray tank are also used for stain, sealer, and lacquer.

Different manufacturers may require a different amount of air pressure for their spray guns. Follow the directions that are recommended for each manufacturer's particular spray gun.

Always test the spray gun on pieces of scrap wood before attempting to spray the cabinet. Sometimes adjustments have to be made before the spray gun is ready to function properly.

Always spray the inside edges of the faceplate parts first because some stain will still get on the top surface.

Spraying is very similar to sanding. Always keep the spray gun moving and never hold it in one spot.

Spray the stain on the faceplate in one direction only, like the arrows in Fig. 6-3. *Never* spray in two directions, like the arrows in Fig. 6-4, because where the stain overlaps, that portion of the faceplate will be darker than the other parts.

After all the cabinets have been stained, spray the cabinets with a heavy coat of sealer. Sealer is clear so it doesn't matter in which direction it is sprayed.

After the sealer has been sprayed on the cabinet and it has dried, sand all surfaces with 400-grit sandpaper. This sandpaper removes the rough surface left by the sealer. The quality of the final finish on the cabinet will depend partially on how well the sealer is sanded with the 400-grit sandpaper.

The sandpaper leaves a fine white dust all over the cabinet. It is not necessary to wipe off all this dust before spraying the lacquer on the cabinet; just blow it off with the air hose.

The same procedure that was used to spray on the sealer is also used to spray on the lacquer.

A heavy coat of lacquer must be sprayed on the cabinet. If a run appears, do not try to wipe it off. Wait until the lacquer dries, slice off the run with a double-edged razor blade, and spray the entire cabinet again.

Never spray a cabinet when another cabinet that has already been sprayed is close by. An overspray will form on the sprayed cabinet that will make the finish feel like sandpaper. Lacquer must be sprayed on very quickly to keep overspray from forming on the parts of the cabinet that have already been sprayed.

The lacquer finish is the final finish; it does not have to be sanded.

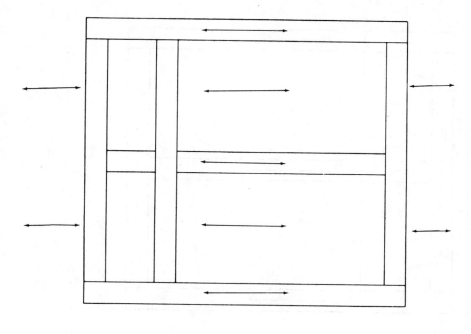

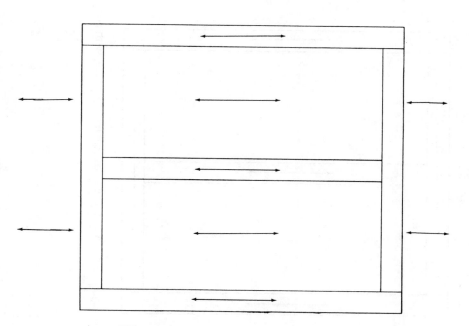

Fig. 6-3   A wall and a base cabinet faceplate, with arrows for spraying directions.

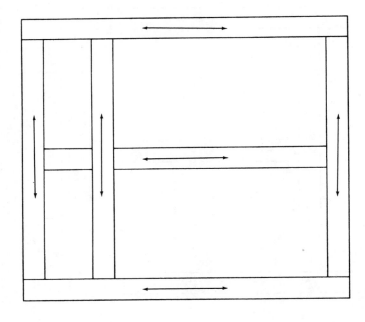

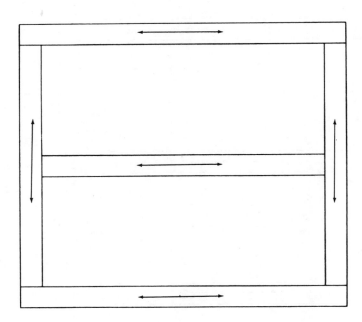

Figure. 6-4 A wall and a base cabinet faceplate, with arrows showing the direction *not* to spray.

chapter 7

LAMINATED PLASTIC TOPS

Laminated plastic is a wear- and heat-resistant plastic that is used to cover kitchen counter tops.

There are two types of laminated plastic tops: post form and edge band.

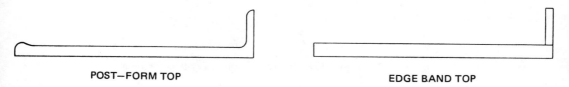

POST—FORM TOP   EDGE BAND TOP

Fig. 7-1   End view of a post-form and an edge-band laminated plastic top.

Post-form tops are built in one piece with the plastic heated and formed to fit the contour of the top. A special post-forming machine must be used to form these tops, which is too expensive and unprofitable for small cabinet manufacturing companies; however, ready-formed and cut-to-size post-form tops can be purchased from companies specializing in building these tops.

Edge-band tops, unlike post-form tops, are usually custom built with a minimum of tools to any width and length by the cabinetmaker.

79

The first step in building an edge-band top is to cut 3/4" thick plywood or particle board to the exact size of the required top to be. The top should be 1-1/2" thick, which is achieved by nailing 2" wide by 3/4" thick wood strips along the edges of the 3/4" thick plywood or particle-board top.

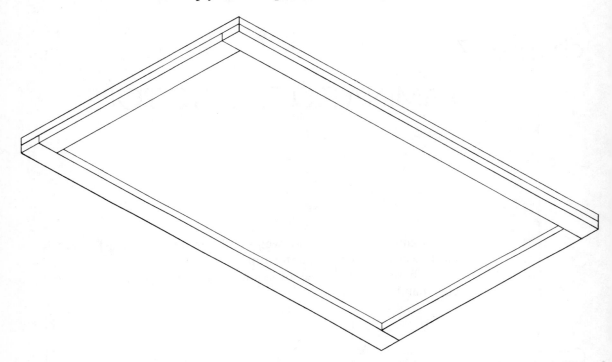

Fig. 7-2   Bottom side of the top showing 2" strips in place.

The top is now ready for the plastic to be applied.

Laminated plastic can be cut on the table saw and it should be cut 1" wider and 1" longer than the top to allow for trimming. The edges are also cut oversize.

The edges are covered first. The front edge is next, and the top is covered last.

The plastic is glued to the top with contact cement, which is a rubber-base glue. It must be applied to both surfaces, the plastic and the top, and allowed to dry completely before it will stick. Once the surfaces are completely dry, they will bond instantly.

The plastic should be glued to the edge of the top first.

Tap the plastic lightly with a rubber hammer to achieve a good bond between the plastic and the top.

Use a veneer trimmer to trim off the excess plastic above the top and bottom edges of the top. Adjust the depth of the cut so that about 1/32″ will be left above the top and bottom surface.

Fig. 7-3 Laminated plastic edge band on each end of the top.

Fig. 7-4 Rubber hammer to tap down plastic.

Fig. 7-5 Trimming plastic with a veneer trimmer.

File off the edges of the plastic that protrude past the front edge of the top.

Apply the plastic to the front edge of the top and trim with the veneer trimmer in the same manner as the two ends.

The 1/32" edge that protrudes above the top and bottom of the top should be sanded down flush with the top and bottom surfaces with a belt sander.

The top is now ready for the plastic to be applied to the top surface, which is done by the same procedure as the edges.

Since the contact cement on the plastic and the top will bond instantly when the two surfaces meet, small strips of wood should be placed on the top to allow the plastic to be positioned correctly before bonding occurs. After the plastic has been placed in the right position, pull the strips out from under the plastic and press it onto the top.

Tap the plastic lightly with a rubber hammer or use a roller to obtain a good bond between the plastic and the top.

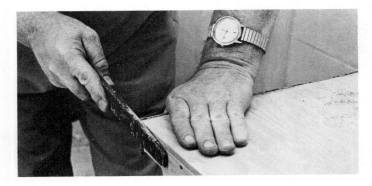

Fig. 7-6   File the ends of the plastic.

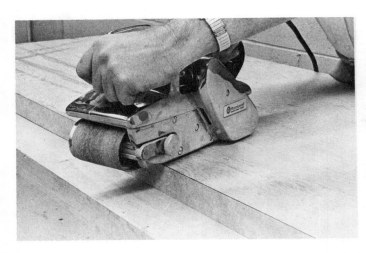

Fig. 7-7   Sanding down the top and bottom edges with a belt sander.

Fig. 7-8 Placing 3/4″ × 3/4″ strips on the top surface of the top to keep the plastic from bonding while lining up the plastic.

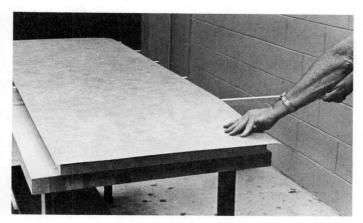

Fig. 7-9 Pulling out strips and pressing down plastic.

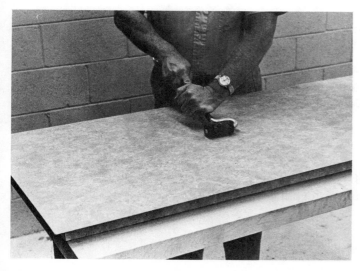

Fig. 7-10 Using a roller on the plastic-covered top.

Like the edges of the top, the excess plastic that protrudes over the top must be trimmed off with a veneer trimmer; however, the edge should be trimmed with a bevel instead of a straight cut. The bevel cut can be made with the same veneer trimmer.

Fig. 7-11   Bevel on the front edge of a laminated plastic top.

The same procedure is followed in building all edge-band tops:

1. Glue the plastic to the ends of the top.
2. File off the protruding ends.
3. Glue the plastic to the front edge of the top.
4. Trim the edges with a veneer trimmer.
5. Sand with a belt sander.
6. Glue the plastic on the top.
7. Trim the edges with a veneer trimmer.

On an L-shape top, the 3/4" plywood or particle board should be cut and joined together like the illustration in Fig. 7-12.

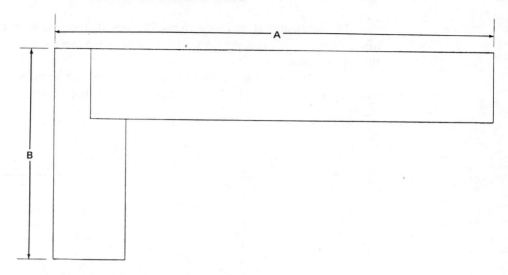

Fig. 7-12   L-shape top, with dimensions.

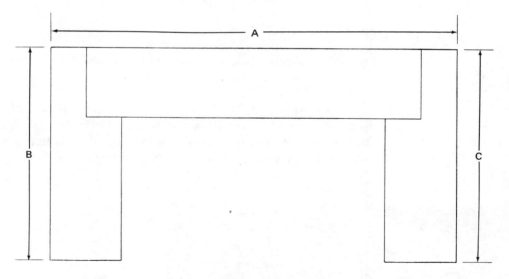

Fig. 7-13   U-shape top, with dimensions.

On a U-shape top, the 3/4″ plywood or particle board should be cut and joined together like the illustration in Fig. 7-13.

If dimension A is less than 144″ and dimensions B and C are each less than 60″, a single piece of plastic can cover the entire top.

If dimension A is more than $144''$ or if dimension B or C is more than $60''$, another piece of plastic must be added to cover the top completely.

If the plastic has to be pieced, it should be pieced where the sink or surface unit will go because less of the seam will show there.

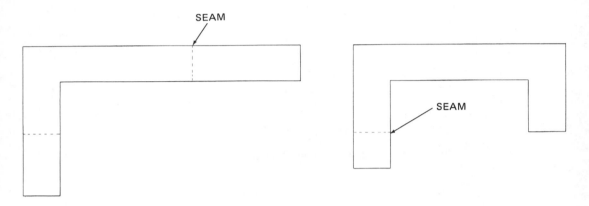

Fig. 7-14   Showing where seams should be on L- and U-shape tops.

To obtain a tight joint when joining two pieces of plastic, each edge must be cut with a router and plastic straightedge guide. One piece of the plastic should overlap the other so that the router will cut through both pieces at the same time.

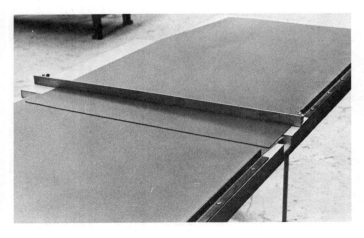

Fig. 7-15   Overlapping plastic on a plastic cutter.

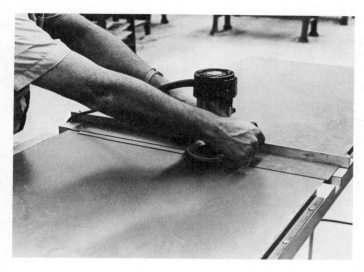

Fig. 7-16 Cutting two overlapping pieces of plastic with a router.

The router cut will leave a very smooth edge on the top surface of the plastic but it will leave a fuzzy edge on the bottom surface. This fuzzy edge should be filed off. *Caution:* Only file the bottom edge; do not file any of the top edge because it will prevent a good fit.

Fig. 7-17 Using a file to remove fuzz from the edges of both pieces of plastic.

Place the two pieces of plastic on the top in the position in which they are to be glued. Test the joint for a tight fit; then make a pencil mark across the top where the two pieces of plastic are to be joined. This is necessary because after the contact cement has been applied to both surfaces, no adjusting can be made.

Apply contact cement on both surfaces: on the plastic and on the top. Wipe off any contact cement that might get on the two edges that are to be joined. After it dries, place several wood strips along the surface of the top; then place the plastic on top of the strips and place the plastic in the right position before the two surfaces are bonded together.

Place the edge of the smaller piece of plastic along the pencil mark on the top, pull out the strips, and bond the two surfaces together.

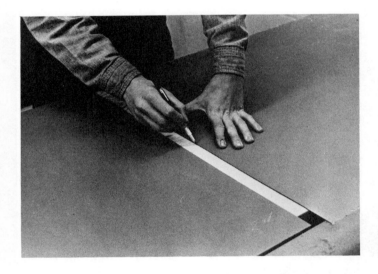

Fig. 7-18   Making a pencil mark on the top where both pieces of plastic go.

Fig. 7-19   Placing 3/4″ X 3/4″ strips on the top surface of the top to keep the plastic from bonding while lining up the plastic.

Fig. 7-20 Placing both pieces of plastic on top of strips.

Fig. 7-21 Lining up a small piece of plastic with a pencil mark.

Fig. 7-22 Pulling strips out from under a small piece of plastic.

Place the edge of the larger piece of plastic next to the edge of the smaller piece that has already been glued and bond about 2″ of the edge of the larger piece of plastic along the edge of the smaller piece.

Leave one wood strip that is under the plastic, about 15″ from the joint; start removing all the other strips and press the plastic down on the top surface.

After all the other strips have been pulled out and the plastic has been bonded to the top, pull out the remaining strip that was left about 15″ from the seam. This will leave a bow in the plastic that can be pressed down, making a very tight joint or seam.

Tap the plastic lightly along all edges with a rubber hammer to ensure a good bond. Trim off the excess plastic with a veneer trimmer. Any contact cement that may be on the top surface of the plastic can be cleaned off with lacquer thinner and a rag.

When a 4″ backsplash is to be used on the top, the backsplash should be built from 4″ wide by 3/4″ thick plywood. The same procedure as for the top is used for gluing the plastic on the backsplash.

The backsplash is attached to the top after the plastic has been applied by wood screws being run up through the top into the backsplash.

Fig. 7-23   Joining the edges of the two pieces of plastic.

Fig. 7-24 Leaving the first strip and removing all the other strips from under the long piece of plastic.

Fig. 7-25 Bow in the plastic after the first strip has been pulled out from under the plastic.

Fig. 7-26 Pressing out bow in the plastic.

Fig. 7-27 Attaching a 4″ backsplash to an edge-band top.

Through the top, drill holes that are slightly larger in diameter than the diameter of the wood screws that are to be used. Always drill from the top side down through the top, never from the bottom side up, to prevent chipping the plastic.

A full backsplash is one that runs from the top of the base cabinets to the bottom of the wall cabinets. The standard distance between is 18". The 18" or full backsplash should be built from 1/4" thick plywood with the front surface covered with plastic.

Unlike the 4" backsplash, the 18" or full backsplash is not attached on the top surface of the top; it is attached from the back edge of the top with wood screws.

Both the 4" backsplash and the full backsplash should be attached to the top before the top is attached to the base cabinets.

Fig. 7-28   Drilling holes from the top side of top for a backsplash.

Fig. 7-29   Attaching an 18" backsplash to a base cabinet top.

chapter 8

HARDWARE INSTALLATION

Hardware installation is the installation of door hinges, door and drawer pulls, drawer guides, and grills.

There are many types and styles of hardware from which to choose. The type or style of the cabinet door, French Provencial, Early American, Spanish, etc., determines the hardware that should be used. Early American hardware should never be used on French Provencial or Spanish doors or vice versa.

The hardware should never be installed on the cabinet until after the finish (stain, paint, etc.) has been applied.

The most common hinge that is used on cabinet doors is the 3/8″ inset hinge. The best 3/8″ inset hinge is the self-closing type, which has a spring built in the hinge that keeps the door closed without using a door catch.

The hinge itself can be used as a guide to locate the other hinges in their proper positions on each end of the door. Place the hinge on the back side of the door where it is flush with both edges of the door and make a small pencil mark on the upper side of the hinge (see Fig. 8-1).

Line up the bottom side of the hinge with the pencil mark and, by using the three holes in the hinge as a guide, punch a small hole in the door back for locating the screws that fasten the hinge to the door.

Fig. 8-1   Locating a hinge by making a pencil mark on the upper side of the hinge.

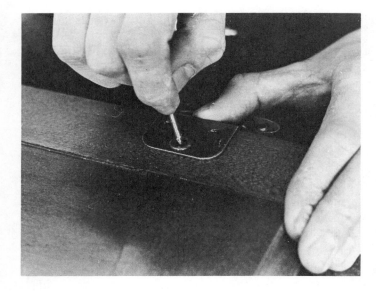

Fig. 8-2   Punching holes for screws.

If a hand screwdriver is used to fasten the hinge to the door, a pilot hole should be drilled where every screw will go. A pilot hole is one that is slightly smaller than the screw that is to be used; this makes it easier to screw the screw in the door.

If an electric or air screwdriver is used, a pilot hole is not necessary, just the small hole made with the punch is sufficient.

If a cabinet has several doors, place them on the cabinet and line them up before attaching them to the cabinet. Use the same procedure to attach the doors to the cabinet that was used to attach the hinges to the doors.

The door pulls are attached to the bottom of a wall cabinet door and the top of a base cabinet door. Drawer pulls should be centered on the drawer front.

Fig. 8-3   Wall and base cabinets with pulls in the right position.

Door and drawer pulls are attached to the doors and drawers by a screw that goes all the way through the door or drawer front into the back of the pull, which is threaded. The holes for these screws should be drilled slightly larger than the diameter of the screw.

When pulls are to be attached to several doors, a jig should be built for locating and drilling the holes for the screws. This will eliminate measuring where each pull will go on each door.

The jig in Fig. 8-4 is handed. It can be changed from left to right by turning over the jig and drilling from the opposite side. *Important:* The holes for the pulls should never be drilled until after the door has been attached to the cabinet. This will eliminate drilling the holes on the wrong end of the door.

There are several different manufacturers of drawer guides. The quality of some may be better than others but the method in

Fig. 8-4   Door-pull-locating jig.

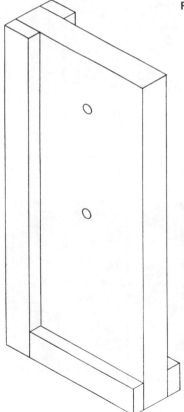

Fig. 8-5   Attaching a monorail to the front of a cabinet.

which they are attached to the drawer and the cabinet are all basically the same.

The monorail drawer guide has two rollers (they are handed, left and right) that are attached to each inside corner of the drawer opening. The monorail is attached to the center of the drawer opening and the back of the cabinet, but do not fasten the monorail to the back of the cabinet until after the drawer has been put in place.

A roller guide that is guided by the monorail is attached to the center of the back end of the drawer. This roller should be located according to the directions that come with the drawer guide because each manufacturer may have a slightly different roller.

After the guide roller has been attached to the back end of the drawer, insert the drawer in the drawer opening. Press the drawer front up flush with the front surface of the faceplate. This will make the back of the monorail move into the position where it is to be attached to the back of the cabinet. Hold the drawer front firmly against the faceplate until after the monorail has been attached to the back of the cabinet.

The side-mounted drawer guide has a guide that is attached to each side of the drawer and each end of the drawer opening.

The guide that attaches to the drawer should be 1-1/8″ from the bottom edge of the drawer.

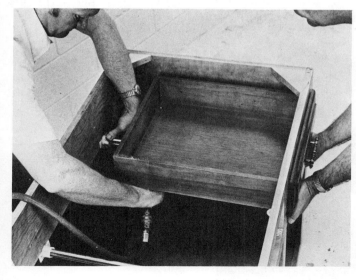

Fig. 8-6   Fastening the back end of the monorail to the back of the cabinet.

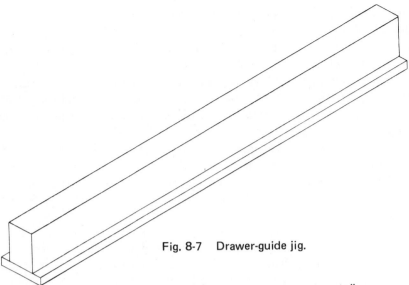

Fig. 8-7   Drawer-guide jig.

Rather than measure the 1-1/8″ from the bottom edge of each drawer separately, build a jig like the one in Fig. 8-7. Use a piece of wood that is 1-1/8″ × 12″ × 3/4″ and nail or staple a 1-1/4″ × 12″ × 1/4″ piece of plywood on one edge of the 1-1/8″ × 12″ × 3/4″ piece of wood. The drawer guide is placed in the right position on the drawer by placing it against the edge of the jig. Punch a small hole in the center of each hole in the drawer guide to locate the positions for the screws that fasten the guide to the drawer. The jig can be removed while the drawer guide is being attached with the screws to the drawer side.

Fig. 8-8   Holding a drawer guide on the drawer side with a jig.

Before the part of the drawer guide that goes on the cabinet can be attached, a 3/4″ thick and 4-1/2″ wide piece of plywood like the one in Fig. 8-9 must be attached to the cabinet.

A 1-1/2″ × 6″ × 1/4″ piece of plywood is fastened on each end of the 3/4″ thick and 4-1/2″ wide plywood so that it can be stapled or nailed from the inside rather than the outside of the cabinet. The total length of the 3/4″ thick by 4-1/2″ wide plywood, which includes the 1-1/2″ × 6″ × 1/4″ piece of plywood on each end, is the same as the distance between the back surface of the faceplate and the back of the cabinet.

The 4-1/2″ wide plywood should be in line with the drawer opening height of the faceplate. The pieces must be paralleled, which means they must be the same distance apart at the back of the cabinet as at the faceplate.

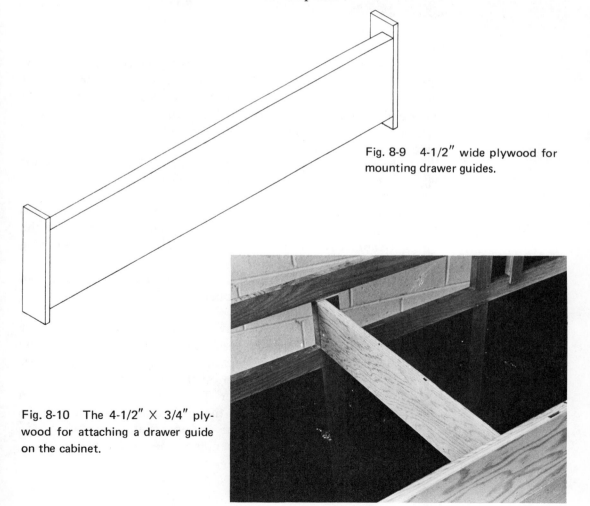

Fig. 8-9   4-1/2″ wide plywood for mounting drawer guides.

Fig. 8-10   The 4-1/2″ × 3/4″ plywood for attaching a drawer guide on the cabinet.

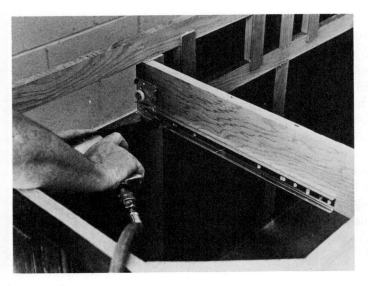

Fig. 8-11 Drawer guide attached
to a cabinet.

The part of the drawer guide that goes on the cabinet is attached to the inside of the drawer opening on the faceplate and is flush with the bottom edge of the 3/4″ thick and 4-1/2″ wide plywood that is attached to the front and back of the cabinet. Leave about 1/16″ clearance between the front surface of the faceplate and the drawer guide.

The drawer is ready to be set in place. If the drawer does not slide easily, one of two things could be wrong.

1. The guides on the cabinet are not paralleled, which means that the distance between the guides in the back of the cabinet is not the same as the width of the drawer opening on the faceplate.
2. The width of the drawer is not exactly 1-1/16″ less than the width of the drawer opening.

A grill is the same as a drawer front but it does not have a drawer attached to it. A grill is used to cover up the opening in the faceplate that is directly below where a sink or surface unit goes or anything else that hangs down on the inside of the cabinet and does not leave room for a drawer. The grill is sometimes called a false drawer. The dimensions of the grill are determined just like the dimensions on a drawer front or door, that is, by adding 5/8″ to the width and height of the opening in the faceplate.

The easiest way to attach a grill to the faceplate is to attach two pieces of 1-1/2″ × 4-7/16″ × 3/4″ wood to the back surface of the grill. Place the grill in position on the faceplate and staple or nail a piece of 1-1/2″ × 7″ × 1/4″ plywood to each 1-1/2″ × 4-7/16″ × 3/4″ piece of wood on the back side of the grill and to the back surface of the faceplate.

The doors, drawers, and grills should not be attached to the cabinet until after the finish (stain, paint, etc.) has been applied.

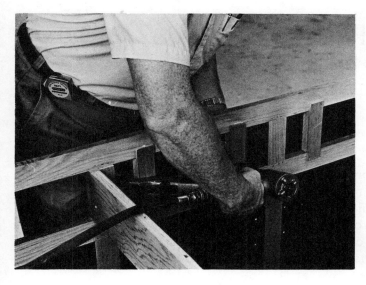

Fig. 8-12 Stapling 1/4″ pieces of the back side of the grill to the cabinet.

chapter 9

BLUEPRINT READING
AND DRAFTING

Blueprint reading, drafting, design, and cabinet layout are all so closely related that with the knowledge of drafting and how to make detail drawings of cabinets, the blueprint reading, design, and cabinet layout will come almost automatically.

The cabinetmaker should be able to make drawings of cabinets that go into much more detail than the drawings made by the architect.

An architect designs all types of buildings including houses and apartments. He makes working drawings that give full directions and information for constructing these buildings. Sometimes the architect will make these drawings himself or he may assign someone else, called a *draftsman*, to make the working drawings of the building that he has designed. Regardless of the type of drawing that he makes, architectural, machine, electrical, cabinet, etc., the person is still referred to as a draftsman.

After the draftsman has completed the working drawings, which are then referred to as the original drawings, copies are made and used so that the original drawings can be filed away for safekeeping. These copies are called *blueprints*.

Blueprints were originally made by reproducing the drawing on a chemically treated paper that made white lines on a blue background. Blueprints are now made on several kinds of special papers that may produce dark blue lines on a light blue background or black lines on a white background. Regardless of the color of the print, they are still referred to as blueprints. A set of blueprints are usually referred to as the "plans."

The location of the cabinets in a house or apartment are shown on the floor plan of the blueprints. The floor plan is a plan view that looks directly down on the object from above (see Fig. 9-1).

Some architects or draftsmen when drawing the plans for a house only show the plan view of the cabinets, while others also show the elevation view, which gives the width and height as well (see Fig. 9-2).

Regardless of whether the architect draws one or both views of the cabinets, a detail drawing must be made to give the cabinet-maker enough information to enable him to build the cabinets. Detail drawings are usually made larger than the plan or elevation view so that all details can be clearly shown.

The draftsman uses a scale to make a drawing to an exact size. When the drawing is made the same size as the part or object, it is called a full-scale drawing. When a larger object cannot be drawn to full size on ordinary paper, a smaller scale must be used. The most commonly used scales for making reduced drawings are $1/8'' = 1'$, $1/4'' = 1'$, $1/2'' = 1'$, $3/4'' = 1'$, and $1'' = 1'$.

Due to the size of cabinets, full-scale drawings would be impractical. Detail drawings of cabinets are usually drawn on a $1''$ scale, which means that $1''$ equals $1'$. *Example:* If the width of a cabinet to be detailed is actually $3'$ or $36''$ wide, it would be drawn $3''$ wide on a $1''$ scale.

If the size of the object that is to be drawn is in exact feet such as $1'$, $3'$, or $10'$, any type of ruler or measuring tape can be used to make the drawing to a certain scale such as $1/4'' = 1'$, $1/2'' = 1'$, or $1'' = 1'$; but when a certain scale, such as $1'' = 1'$, is used and the part that is to be drawn is $2''$ wide or $4''$ wide, etc., an architect's scale must be used to determine what portion of the inch is $2''$ or $4''$, etc.

The most common architect's scale is a triangular-shaped scale that has 11 different scales on it: full scale or $12'' = 1'$, $3'' = 1'$, $1\text{-}1/2'' = 1'$, $1'' = 1'$, $3/4'' = 1'$, $1/2'' = 1'$, $3/8'' = 1'$, $1/4'' = 1'$, $3/16'' = 1'$, $1/8'' = 1'$, and $3/32'' = 1'$ (see Fig. 9-3).

Each of the different scales on the architect's scale is divided into parts that represent the inches and fractions of an inch of the foot.

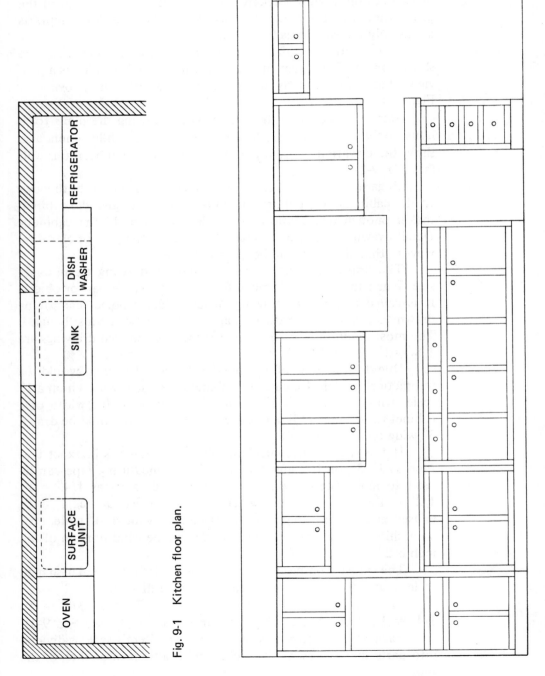

Fig. 9-1   Kitchen floor plan.

Fig. 9-2   Elevation view of kitchen cabinets.

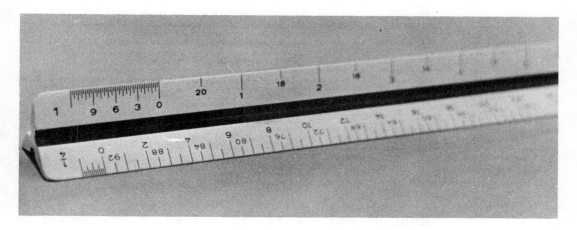

Fig. 9-3   Architect's scale.

Figure 9-4 is the 1″ = 1′ scale. From 0 to 1 actually measures
an inch but on the 1″ = 1′ scale it represents 12″ or 1′. The 3, 6,
and 9 on the scale represent 3″, 6″, and 9″, respectively, on the
1″ scale. The scale is too small to put all the figures such as 1/4″,
1/2″, and 1″ on it but each little line represents 1/4″. If the 1″
scale was larger, it would be marked like Fig. 9-5.

The scale used to make the drawing should always be indicated and the dimensions shown on the drawing should be the

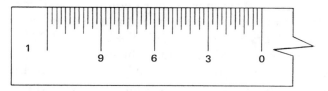

Fig. 9-4   1′ on an architect's scale.

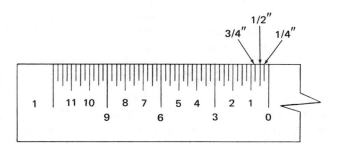

Fig. 9-5   1/4″, 1/2″, and 3/4″ on
the 1″ = 1′ scale.

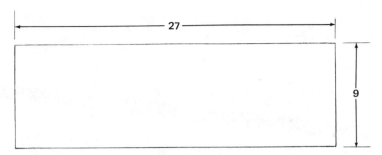

Fig. 9-6   9″ X 27″ rectangle at 1″ scale.

actual dimensions of the object and not the dimensions of the drawing (see Fig. 9-6).

On architectural drawings or blueprints, all dimensions are indicated in feet and inches: 2′3″, 8′9″, 13′4″, etc. On cabinet detail drawings, all dimensions, regardless of the size, are indicated in inches: 27″, 105″, 160″, etc. Since the dimensions on all cabinet detail drawings are indicated in inches, the inch symbol (″) can be eliminated.

There are certain basic steps that should be followed before a drawing can be made and there are also certain basic tools, equipment, and supplies that are required before a drawing can be made.

The different kinds of drafting tools, equipment, and supplies that are available for the draftsman are too numerous to mention, but the basics are the drawing board, T square, triangle, architect's scale, pencil, pencil sharpener, eraser, erasing shield, drafting powder, drafting brush, drawing paper, and masking tape.

A 24″ X 36″ drawing board, 36″ T square, and 22″ X 34″ drawing paper are best suited for detail cabinet drawing.

The 22″ X 34″ drawing paper should be placed on the 24″ X 36″ drawing board so that there will be a 1″ space between the paper and the edge of the drawing board on all four sides. The T square should be used to line up the paper parallel with the edge of the drawing board. Tape down the two top corners of the paper to the drawing board with masking tape. When a large piece of drawing paper is used, all four corners should be taped down.

A mechanical drafting pencil with 2H lead is preferred for cabinet detail drawing. A mechanical drafting pencil has a threaded or slip chuck that makes changing the lead or extending the right amount of lead past the end of the pencil very easy (see Fig. 9-9).

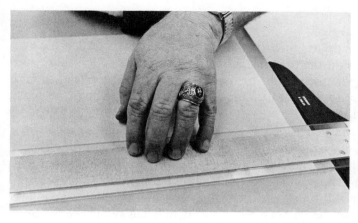

Fig. 9-7 Lining up paper on a drawing board.

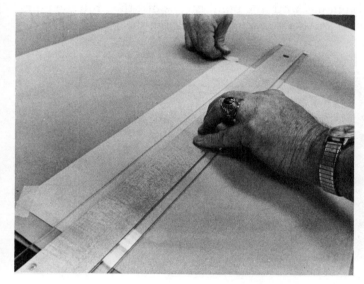

Fig. 9-8 Taping down paper.

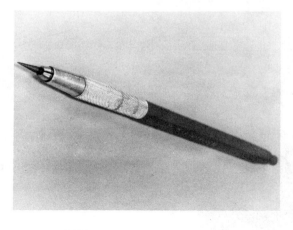

Fig. 9-9 Mechanical pencil.

107

A sharp point must be kept on the pencil to obtain a clean and clear line on the drawing. Either a mechanical pencil sharpener or a sandpaper pad should be used. About 3/8″ of the lead should extend out past the end of the pencil after sharpening (see Figs. 9-10, -11, -12).

Never sharpen a pencil over the drawing board, and always wipe the lead with a cloth to remove the fine dust from the point.

Both the mechanical pencil sharpener and the sandpaper pad will sharpen the pencil lead to such a fine point that a small portion of the point will break off when the first line is drawn. To eliminate this from happening on the drawing, always make a short line on a scratch pad until the point breaks off; then rub the point back and forth on the scratch pad, rotating the pencil, until the broken edge is smooth (see Figs. 9-13, -14).

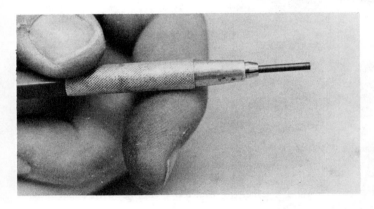

Fig. 9-10 A mechanical pencil with 3/8″ of lead extending past the pencil end.

Fig. 9-11 A mechanical pencil sharpener.

Fig. 9-12   Sanding pad.

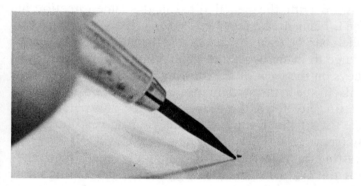

Fig. 9-13   Breaking a pencil point on a scratch pad.

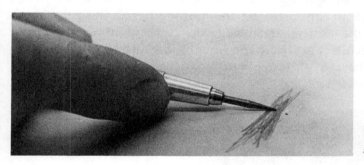

Fig. 9-14   Smoothing a pencil point and edge on a scratch pad.

Horizontal lines are drawn by using the upper edge of the T-square blade as a straightedge and guide. Hold the head of the T square against the left edge of the drawing board with the left hand and move it up and down the edge of the drawing board to the desired position. *Note:* This procedure should be reversed for left-handed persons. The head of the T square should be held against the right edge of the drawing board with the right hand.

109

While holding the T square with the left hand (right hand for left-handed persons), hold the pencil with the other hand and tilt the pencil in the same direction in which the line is being drawn. Rotate the pencil with the thumb and forefinger as the line is being drawn; this prevents the point from wearing down on one edge. Rotating the pencil will make the point wear evenly and keep a uniform and clean line (see Fig. 9-15).

Vertical lines are drawn by using a triangle for a straightedge and guide. With the T square being held in the same method as when drawing horizontal lines, the triangle is placed on the top edge of the T-square blade with the vertical edge of the triangle toward the left (right for left-handed persons). Vertical lines should be drawn upward with the pencil tilted in the same direction in which the line is being drawn (see Fig. 9-16).

A parallel bar is used by many draftsmen when they are working on large drawing boards. A guide cord running through a series of pulleys on the back of the drawing board and through the straightedge itself keeps the straightedge in a parallel position even when moved up and down the drawing board. The parallel bar eliminates the use of the T square but the triangle is still used in the same way (see Fig. 9-17).

The drafting machine is more commonly used than the parallel bar or the T square. The drafting machine has a horizontal and a vertical straightedge that always remains horizontal or vertical when moved to any place on the drawing board. Both the horizontal and the vertical straightedge has a scale imprinted on it just like the architect's scale. The use of a drafting machine can eliminate the use of the T square, triangle, and the architect's scale (see Fig. 9-18).

Fig. 9-15 Using a T square and drawing with pencil.

Fig. 9-16 Using a triangle on a T square and drawing a vertical line.

Fig. 9-17 Parallel bar.

Fig. 9-18 Drafting machine.

Regardless of whether a T square, parallel bar, or a drafting machine is used on a drawing board, the same drafting techniques are used on each one.

To understand best how to draw kitchen cabinets is to understand first where they are to be installed after they are built. The cabinets should be drawn to scale and in the same position as they will be when they are installed.

The first step in drawing a kitchen cabinet is to draw two horizontal lines, the bottom one representing the floor of a room and the top one representing the ceiling. The ceiling height of the

Fig. 9-19   Floor and ceiling lines.

rooms in most houses is 8' or 96", therefore, making the two lines 8" apart when drawn at 1" scale (1" = 1') (see Fig. 9-19).

Since the base cabinets sit on the floor, they should be drawn in the same position. Wall cabinets are fastened to the wall with the tops of the wall cabinets exactly 7' from the floor or 1' from the ceiling. They should be drawn in the same position.

Both wall and base cabinets have a standard height but either one can be built to any width. The standard wall cabinet is 30" high. The only ones that are different are the ones over a stove or refrigerator. The standard base cabinet is 34-1/2" high. When the 1-1/2" thick counter top is placed on top of the 34-1/2" high base cabinet, the counter top will be 36" high.

The number of doors that are added to both wall and base cabinets are determined by the width of the cabinet. The following rule should be followed:

$$9" \text{ to } 24" = 1 \text{ door}$$
$$24" \text{ to } 42" = 2 \text{ doors}$$
$$42" \text{ to } 60" = 3 \text{ doors}$$
$$60" \text{ to } 78" = 4 \text{ doors}$$
$$78" \text{ to } 96" = 5 \text{ doors}$$

The following steps should be taken to draw a 36" wide wall cabinet and a 36" wide base cabinet at 1" scale (1" = 1').

Using the 1" scale, measure along the floor line (bottom line) 36" (0 to 3 on the architect's scale), make a light mark on the floor line at 0 and 3, and then use the triangle to draw a light line from the two marks, which were at 0 and 3, to the ceiling (top line). *Note:* These light lines are called *construction lines* and they should be drawn very lightly because parts of these lines will later be erased.

Measure up from the floor line (bottom line) 34-1/2" and make a light mark on the left vertical line. Measure down from the

Fig. 9-20   Making marks at 0 and 3 on an architect's scale.

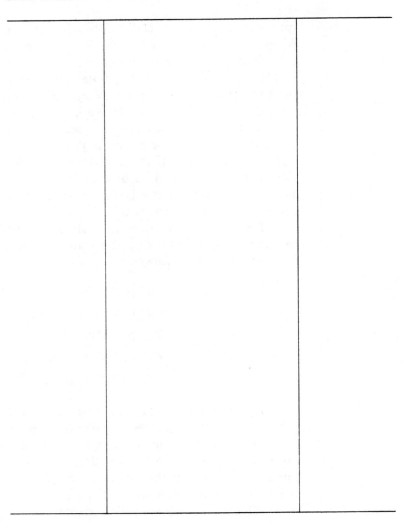

Fig. 9-21   Drawing two vertical lines.

ceiling line (top line) 12″, make a light mark, and then measure
down from that mark 30″ and make another light mark.

From the mark on the left vertical line that is 12″ down from
the ceiling, draw a horizontal line over to the right vertical line.
From the mark on the left vertical line that is 30″ down from the
first mark, draw a horizontal line over to the right vertical line.
From the mark on the left vertical line that is 34-1/2″ from the
floor, draw a horizontal line over to the right vertical line.

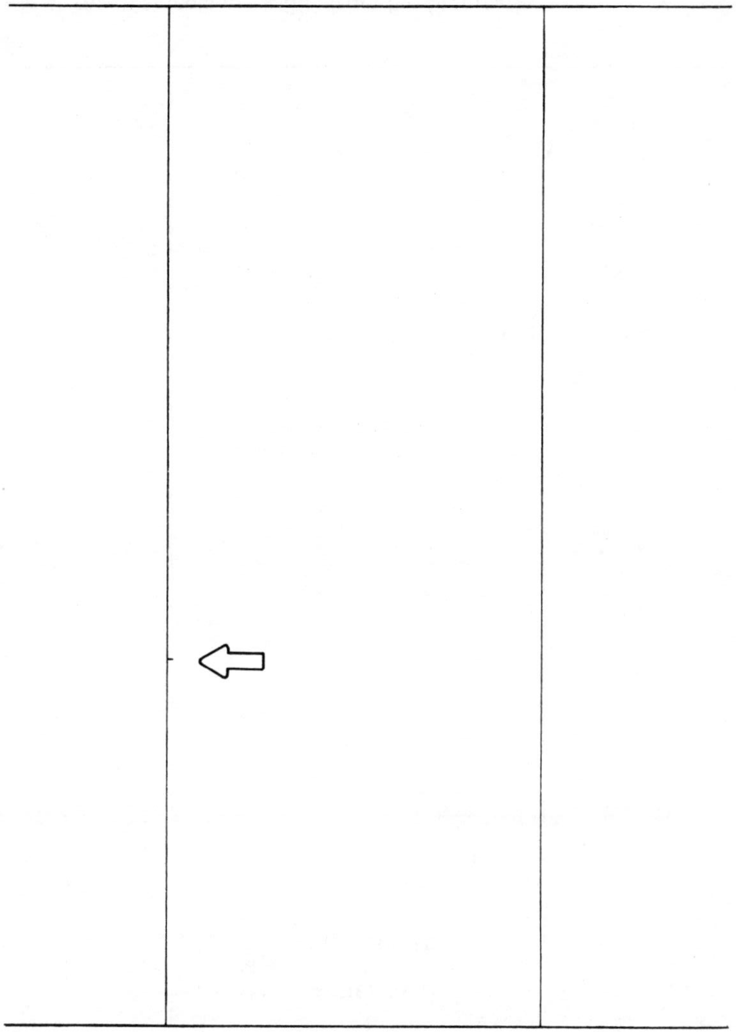

MARK ALREADY
MADE FOR BASE

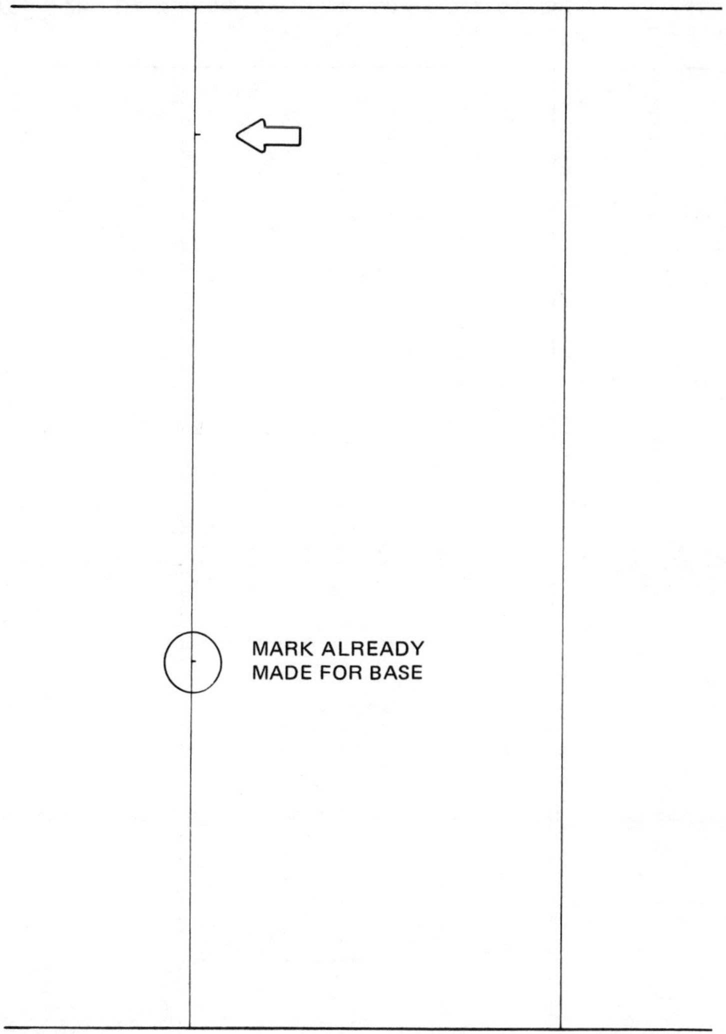

Fig. 9-23   Making a mark 12″ from the ceiling.

Fig. 9-22   Making marks on vertical lines for base cabinets.

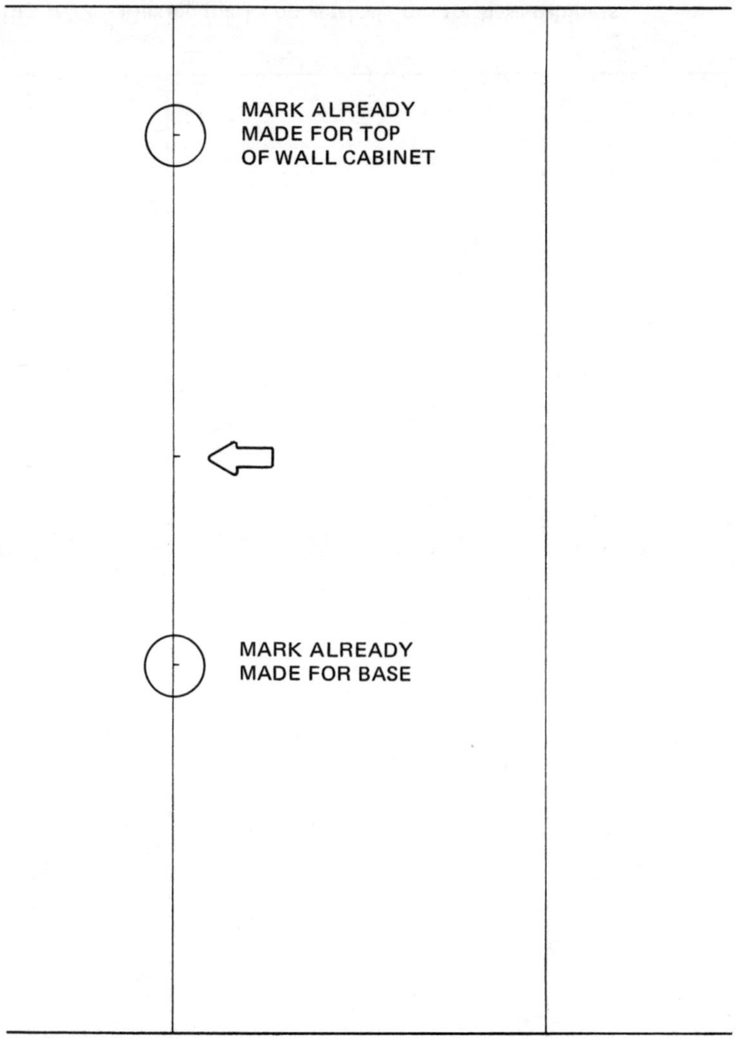

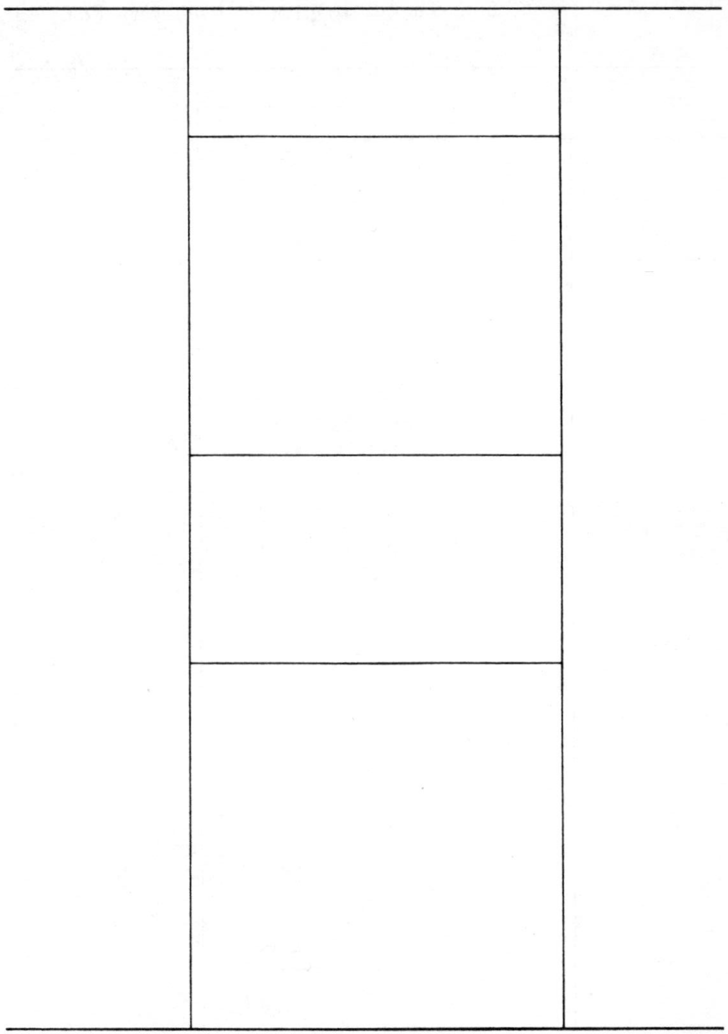

Fig. 9-25   Drawing horizontal lines on the base cabinet.

MARK ALREADY
MADE FOR TOP
OF WALL CABINET

MARK ALREADY
MADE FOR BASE

Fig. 9-24   Making a mark 30″ from the first mark.

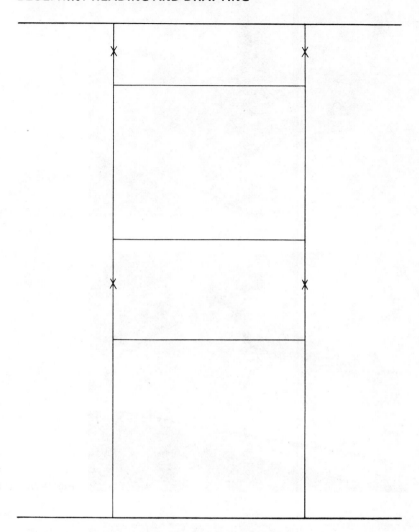

Fig. 9-26 "X" marks on lines to be taken out.

Erase all the lines in Fig. 9-26 that have an "X" mark on them.

Use an erasing shield to keep from erasing the permanent lines of the drawing. An erasing shield has several odd-shaped holes in it that allow a line to be erased to an exact point.

Use a drafting brush to brush away all the eraser shavings.

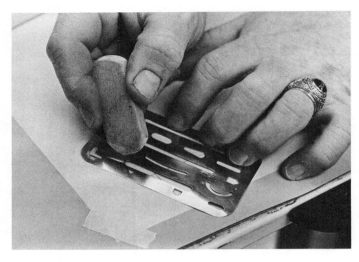

Fig. 9-27   Using an erasing shield.

Fig. 9-28   Using a drafting brush.

Fig. 9-29   Using drafting powder.

To help keep the drawing clean, sprinkle drafting powder over the drawing. This will help to eliminate smudge marks usually caused by the drafting tools sliding across the paper.

Go over the light lines that are left and make them darker. Be sure to follow the same lines exactly.

The lines that are left form the *outline* of the wall and base cabinet. The lines representing the faceplate parts of the cabinet can now be added to make the drawing look like the front view of the real cabinet. The front view of the cabinets is the only view that is necessary because the depth of the wall cabinet, which is

Fig. 9-30   Showing dark finish lines.

12″, is standard and the depth of the base cabinet, which is 24″, is also standard. All the inside parts of the cabinets, which were discussed in Chapter 2, are also standard.

From the floor line (bottom line), measure up 4″ on the left side of the base cabinet outline and make a light mark. Draw a horizontal line from the light mark to the right side of the base cabinet outline. This line represents the toeboard of the base cabinet.

All the faceplate parts, the stiles, rails, and mullions, are 2″ wide. The stiles are the outside vertical parts on both the wall and

Fig. 9-31   Wall and base cabinets.

the base faceplate. The rails are the horizontal parts and the mullions are the vertical parts between the left and right stiles.

Draw the stiles from the bottom to the top of the wall cabinet and from the top of the toeboard line to the *top* of the base cabinet. Draw the top and bottom rails of the wall cabinet; then draw a mullion in the center of the wall cabinet. Draw the top and bottom rails of the base cabinet. Draw a center rail 4-1/2" down from the bottom of the top rail. This 4-1/2" space is for the drawers. Draw a mullion in the center of the base cabinet between the bottom rail and the center rail and between the center rail and the top rail (see Fig. 9-31).

Even though the detail drawings of cabinets are drawn to scale, small parts that are 1/8", 1/4", 1/2", etc., would be im-

Fig. 9-32   Extension lines for dimensions.

EXTENSION LINES

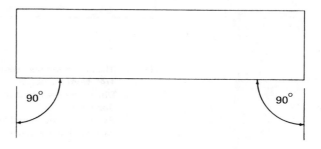

(1) Extension lines must be drawn at 90 degrees to the surface that is dimensioned.

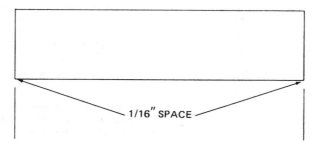

(2) Leave a 1/16" space between the object and the extension lines.

possible to draw with any degree of accuracy, therefore making it impossible to measure these drawings with an architect's scale and obtain an accurate measurement. Dimensions are added to the drawing to give the exact size of the object that has been drawn.

The standard rules for dimensioning can be shown best by observing Figs. 9-32, -33, and -34.

The same principles of drawing that were used throughout this chapter are used to make all drawings.

Fig. 9-33   Dimension lines.

DIMENSION LINES

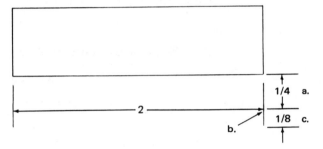

(1) a. The dimension lines should be at least 1/4″ from the object.
     b. Dimension lines must touch the extension lines.
     c. Extension lines should extend 1/8″ past the dimension line.

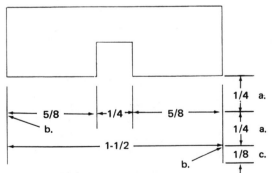

(2) When several dimension lines are parallel to each other, they should be the same distance apart. (a)

The extension lines must still extend 1/8″ past the last dimension line. (c)

Arrows should be slim ◄——— , not ◄——

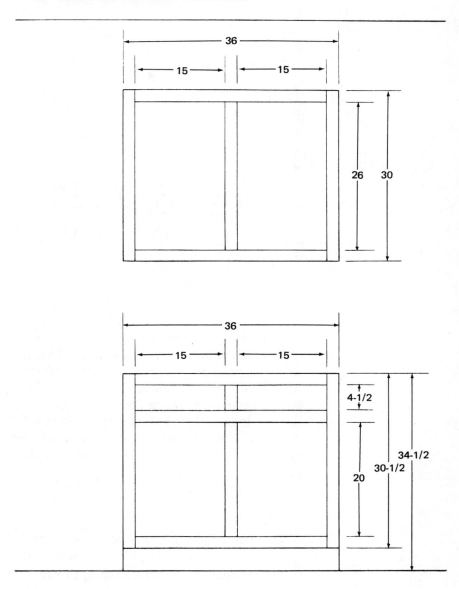

Fig. 9-34   Wall and base cabinets with dimensions.

chapter 10

KITCHEN DESIGN
AND CABINET LAYOUT

Before a draftsman attempts to design and draw a complete kitchen, he should be familiar with all minimum requirements for cabinets, such as the square footage of the shelves, counter top space, and drawers. These minimum requirements vary according to the type of dwelling (house or apartment), the size, and the type of loan if the building is to be financed. The Federal Housing Administration (FHA) has set up the following minimum requirements that will usually satisfy any bank or other lending institution:

1. Houses:
   (a) Total shelving in wall and base cabinets, 50 square feet with not less than 20 square feet in wall or base cabinets.
   (b) Minimum counter top area, 11 square feet.
   (c) Minimum drawer area, 11 square feet.
2. One-bedroom and two-bedroom apartments with kitchen area over 60 square feet:
   (a) Total shelving in wall and base cabinets, 48 square feet with not less than 18 square feet in wall or base cabinets.
   (b) Minimum counter top area, 10 square feet.
   (c) Minimum drawer area, 8 square feet.

3. Three- and four-bedroom apartments with kitchen area over 60 square feet:
   (a) Total shelving in wall and base cabinets, 54 square feet with not less than 20 square feet in wall or base cabinets.
   (b) Minimum counter top area, 12 square feet.
   (c) Minimum drawer area, 10 square feet.
4. No-bedroom apartment with 30 to 60 square feet of kitchenette area:
   (a) Total shelving in wall and base cabinets, 24 square feet with not less than 10 square feet in wall or base cabinets.
   (b) Minimum counter top area, 5 square feet.
   (c) Minimum drawer area, 4 square feet.
5. One-bedroom apartment with 30 to 60 square feet of kitchenette area:
   (a) Total shelving in wall and base cabinets, 30 square feet with not less than 12 square feet in wall or base cabinets.
   (b) Minimum counter top area, 6 square feet.
   (c) Minimum drawer area, 5 square feet.

Area occupied by sink basin and by cooking units shall not be included in minimum counter top area.

Usable storage space in cooking ranges, when provided in the form of drawers or shelving, may be included in the minimum shelf area.

Shelf area of revolving base shelves (lazy Susan) may be considered as twice its actual area in determining required shelf area provided clear width of opening is at least 8-1/2".

Drawer area may be substituted for not more than 25% of required base shelf area.

Before a draftsman attempts to design and draw a complete kitchen, he should also be familiar with the cabinets other than the standard wall and base cabinet, such as the Vent-A-Hood cabinet, refrigerator cabinet, corner cabinet, and oven cabinet, as well as space for the dishwasher, that are used to complete a kitchen.

A Vent-A-Hood is a vented hood with an exhaust fan that removes grease, smoke, and odor coming from the stove. The Vent-A-Hood is attached to the bottom of a cabinet that is set directly above the stove. The most common size is 36" wide. Since the Vent-A-Hood is attached to the bottom of a cabinet, this cabinet should

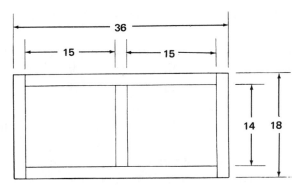

Fig. 10-1 Vent-A-Hood cabinet, with dimensions.

be 36″ wide and 18″ high. It is referred to as a Vent-A-Hood cabinet (see Fig. 10-1).

The space that is usually left for a refrigerator is 36″ wide by 72″ high. The cabinet over a refrigerator should be 36″ wide by 12″ high. It is referred to as a refrigerator cabinet (see Fig. 10-2).

An oven cabinet is one that houses a built-in oven and extends from the floor up to the top of the wall cabinets. It has a toeboard like a base cabinet and doors below and above the built-in oven. The oven cabinet could be referred to as a combination base and wall cabinet but since it sits on the floor like a base cabinet, it is more closely related to the base cabinet.

The only thing that is standard on an oven cabinet is the height, which is 84″. The opening for the built-in oven will vary with every make and model oven, which also makes the width of the oven cabinet vary. The exact opening for a built-in oven can be obtained from the manufacturer of the oven that is to be used. This opening size must be known before the draftsman can proceed with the designing and drawing of the kitchen (see Fig. 10-3).

The depth of the oven cabinet should be 25″ so that the plastic top, which is 25″ wide, will fit flush with the front and back of the cabinet (see Fig. 10-4).

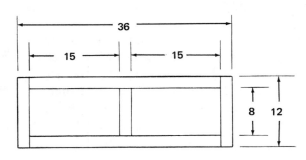

Fig. 10-2 Refrigerator cabinet, with dimensions.

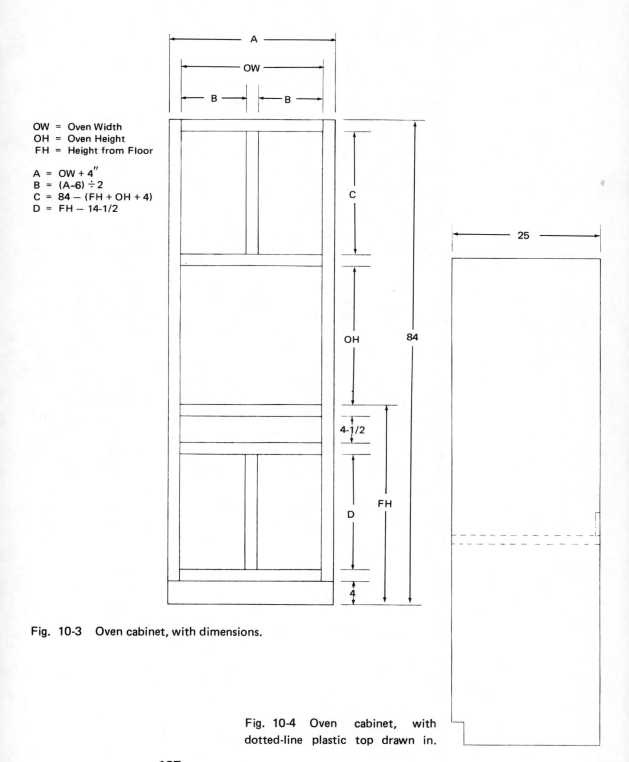

OW = Oven Width
OH = Oven Height
FH = Height from Floor

A = OW + 4″
B = (A–6) ÷ 2
C = 84 – (FH + OH + 4)
D = FH – 14-1/2

Fig. 10-3   Oven cabinet, with dimensions.

Fig. 10-4   Oven cabinet, with dotted-line plastic top drawn in.

127

The dishwasher is usually located close to the sink and unlike the Vent-A-Hood, refrigerator, and oven the dishwasher does not require a special cabinet. An opening is left between two base cabinets with the plastic counter top extending across the top of the dishwasher opening.

The opening for a 24″ dishwasher is 24-1/2″ wide and 34-1/2″ high (the same height as the base cabinet) (see Fig. 10-5).

When cabinets make a 90-degree turn like the L-shape kitchen in Fig. 10-6 and the U-shape kitchen in Fig. 10-7, corner cabinets must be used to make these turns.

One type of corner cabinet is shown in Fig. 10-8. Lazy Susan shelves can also be installed inside this type of wall and base corner cabinet.

The most common corner wall or base cabinet is built just like any other wall or base cabinet except for a change in the faceplate. The faceplate is built in such a way as to make the end of a standard cabinet butt into the front of this cabinet, thus making a 90-degree turn (see Fig. 10-9).

Since the depth of a standard wall cabinet is 12″, the corner cabinet faceplate must be built with a 3″ wide mullion located 14″ from the end. The end of the other cabinet that is butting against this corner cabinet will also butt against the 3″ wide mull and leave 2″ of the mull exposed. The 3″ wide mull should extend from the top to the bottom of the faceplate so that the 2″ that is exposed will look like a stile (see Figs. 10-10 and 10-11).

Fig. 10-5   Dishwasher space.

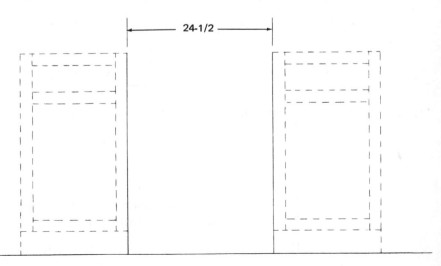

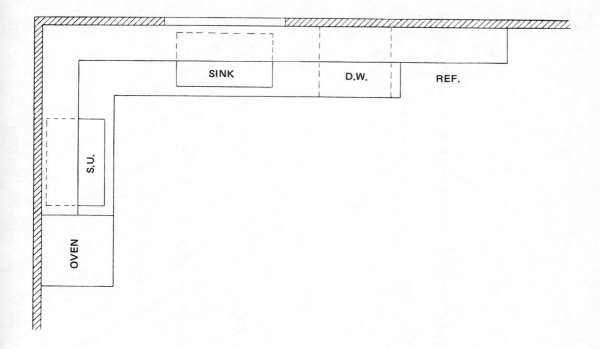

Fig. 10-6   Plan view of an L-shape kitchen.

Fig. 10-7   Plan view of a U-shape kitchen.

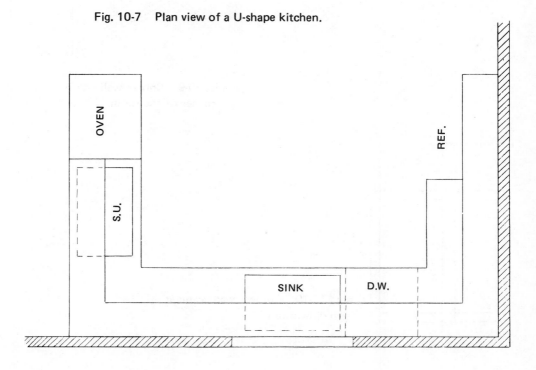

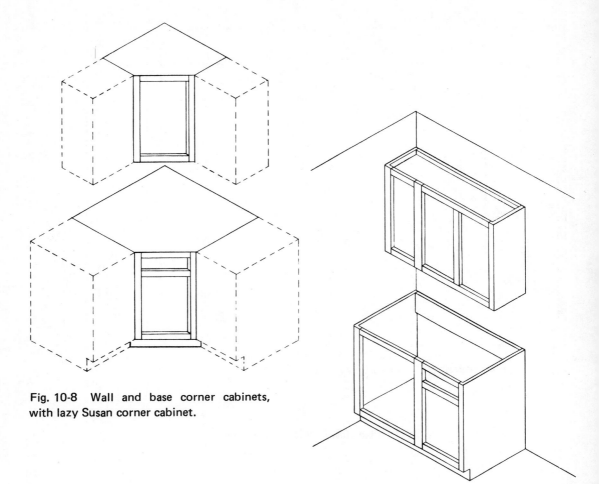

Fig. 10-8 Wall and base corner cabinets, with lazy Susan corner cabinet.

Fig. 10-9 Corner wall and base cabinets in a corner of the room.

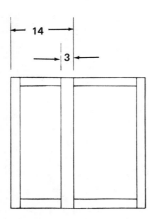

Fig. 10-10 Corner wall cabinet, with dimensions.

130

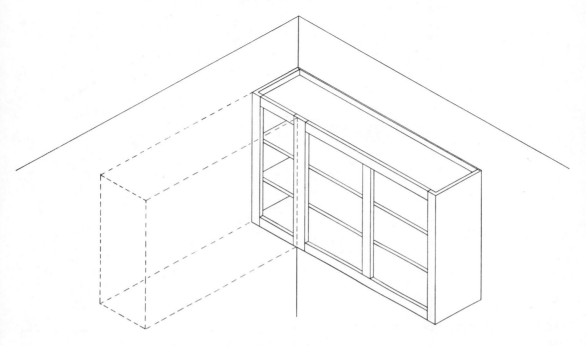

Fig. 10-11   Cabinet butting into a corner wall cabinet.

The corner base cabinet faceplate is built similarly to the corner wall cabinet faceplate except for the location of the 3″ wide mull. Since the depth of a standard base cabinet is 24″, the 3″ wide mull is located 26″ from the end.

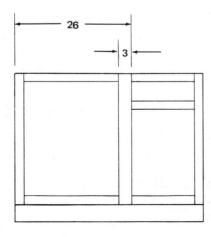

Fig. 10-12   Corner base cabinet, with dimensions.

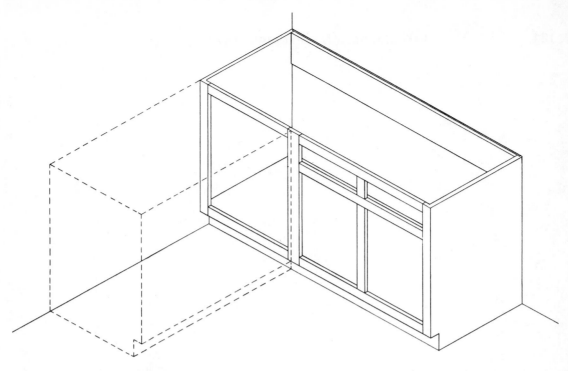

Fig. 10-13 Cabinet butting into a corner
base cabinet.

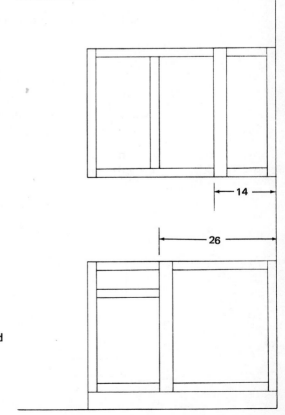

Fig. 10-14 Wall and base blind
ends, with dimensions.

132

All corner cabinets are handed (left or right) and they should be referred to as left or right corner wall cabinets or left or right corner base cabinets.

The ends of the corner cabinets that are covered up or hidden when the other cabinets butt into them are referred to as blind ends.

Corner cabinets, both wall and base, can be built at any width but the blind ends must always remain the same (see Fig. 10-14).

Like the standard wall and base cabinet, the number of doors that are added to a corner wall or base cabinet is determined by the width of the cabinet, which includes the blind end. The following rule should be followed.

Corner Wall Cabinets

24″ to 36″ = 1 door
36″ to 54″ = 2 doors
54″ to 72″ = 3 doors
72″ to 96″ = 4 doors

Corner Base Cabinets

36″ to 48″ = 1 door
48″ to 66″ = 2 doors
66″ to 84″ = 3 doors
84″ to 96″ = 4 doors

In addition to the overall dimensions and the exact location of the cabinets, there are five other dimensions that must be known before a kitchen can be designed—ceiling height, distance from top of windows to ceiling, oven opening, window width, and the distance from the window to the corner of the room.

Since the plan view is a view looking down on an object and an elevation view shows the width and height, a kitchen layout drawing should show both the plan view and the elevation view on the same drawing. This is done by visualizing the kitchen or room as if it were a cardboard box with all four corners cut and the sides folded down, the bottom of the box representing the floor and the four sides representing the four walls. By using the exact dimensions of the kitchen, the plan view and elevation view of the room should be drawn at 1″ scale (1″ = 1′0″) (see Figs. 10-15 and 10-16).

The floor plan and the location of all doors and windows should first be drawn on the floor plan view. The doors and windows should then be drawn in their proper location on the elevation

Fig. 10-15   Box view of room.

Fig. 10-16   Floor plan of a U-shape kitchen.

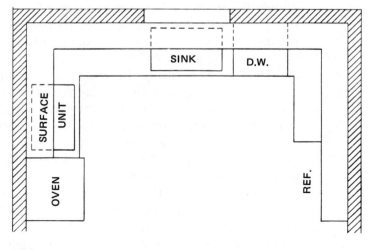

view. The outline (stiles, rails, and mulls haven't been added) of all cabinets that must be built to a standard or certain size such as the oven, refrigerator, and Vent-A-Hood cabinets and the location of the dishwasher should be drawn next. Then draw the outline of the cabinets in the space where cabinets are required between the doors and the windows and the outline of the other cabinets that have already been drawn.

Fig. 10-17 Drawing of the floor plan, plan view, and elevation view on a box view.

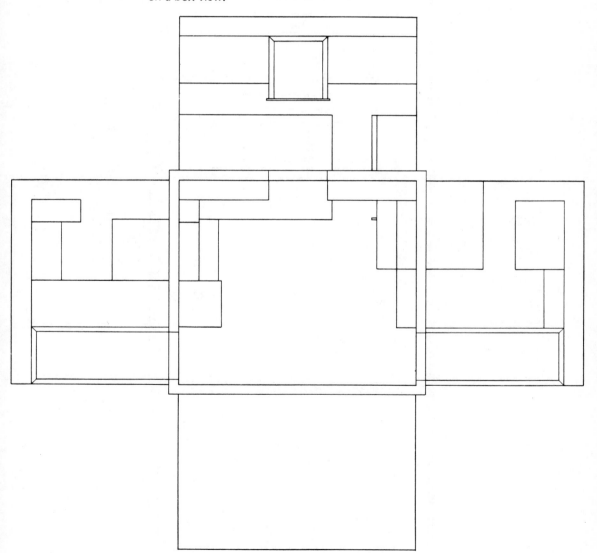

Before adding the faceplate parts (stiles, rails, and mulls) to the cabinet outlines, find the center line of the sink location, which is usually the same as the center line of the window; then draw a 2″ wide mull. This dimension can vary but it should never be less than 15″ because a double-bowl sink is 32″ wide.

After the sink has been located, use the rule to determine how many doors to add according to the width of the cabinet; then add all other faceplate parts to the cabinet outlines.

Fig. 10-18   Box view of a full kitchen.

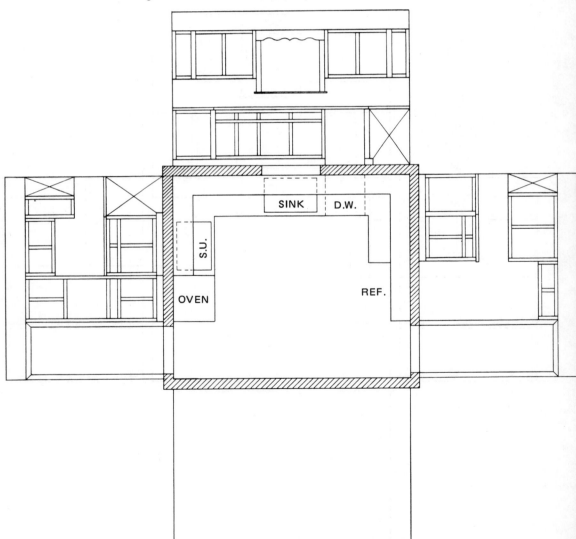

By using the same floor plan as in Fig. 10-16 and combining the plan view and the elevation view, the complete kitchen layout should be drawn just like Fig. 10-18.

Fig. 10-19   Drawing of a cabinet, with a list of all component parts.

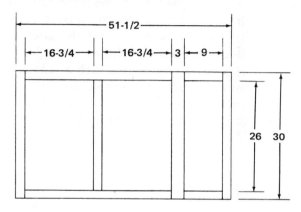

FACE PLATE				
NO.	WIDTH	LENGTH	THICK	PART
2	2	30	3/4	STILES
2	2	37	3/4	RAILS
2	2	10-1/2	3/4	RAILS
1	2	27-1/2	3/4	MULL
1	3	30	3/4	MULL

CABINET					DOORS				
NO.	WIDTH	LENGTH	THICK	PART	NO.	WIDTH	LENGTH	THICK	PART
1	11-15/16	30	7/8	RAISED PANEL END	2	17-3/8	26-5/8	7/8	Raised Panel Doors
1	11-15/16	30	3/4	FIR PLYWOOD END					
4	11	50-3/16	3/4	FIR PLYWOOD SHELVES	4	2-1/4	26-5/8	7/8	STILES
1	30	50-7/8	1/4	FIR PLYWOOD BACK	4	2-1/4	13-5/8	7/8	RAILS
					2	13-5/8	22-7/8	9/16	PANELS

Each individual cabinet should now be drawn, showing the exact location and dimensions of all faceplate parts. A bill of material list giving the exact dimensions of all faceplate parts and a bill of material list giving the exact dimension of all the cabinet components should also be included (see Fig. 10-19).

If a blueprint of the floor plan is not available and the cabinet draftsman has to design his own kitchen, the same basic principles that were used to lay out the kitchen from the blueprint are also used to design and draw the kitchen from the draftsman's design. The standard cabinets such as the refrigerator, Vent-A-Hood, and oven cabinet; the dishwasher space; the windows; and the doors are drawn in first; then the other wall and base cabinets are drawn to fill up the space requiring cabinets.

chapter 11

COMPUTATION OF COMPONENT PARTS

The average kitchen uses about 10 to 15 cabinets to fill the space requiring cabinets. Each cabinet must be built individually from the many component parts that are required to build each one.

This chapter will help to determine the exact dimensions of the faceplate parts and all other component parts required to build the cabinet. All of these parts are computed from the width or the *A* dimension of the required cabinet.

Every type and size of cabinet that could be used in any kitchen are included in this chapter. The type to be used is determined by the location of the required cabinet and the width of the cabinet used to fill the space requiring cabinets.

Chapter 2 covered the three most common ways to attach the wall cabinet and base cabinet ends to the faceplate: the butt joint, the dado and lip joint, and the lock joint.

When using the butt joint and the dado and lip joint, all the component parts are the same with the exception of the width of the wall and base ends.

When using the butt joint, the width of the wall end is 11-1/4″ and the width of the base end is 23-1/4″.

When using the dado and lip joint, the width of the wall end is 11-1/2″ and the width of the base end is 23-1/2″.

When using the lock joint, the width of the wall end is 11-15/16″ and the width of the base end is 23-15/16″ but all the other component parts are computed differently from the butt or dado and lip joint.

When using the butt or dado and lip joint, all wall and base ends are 3/4″ thick.

Raised-panel or Spanish wall or base ends can be used when the lock joint is used and these ends are 7/8″ thick. The raised-panel or Spanish end is only used as a finished or exposed end. The end of the cabinet that butts against the wall or another cabinet, which is referred to as the unfinished end, has a 3/4″ thick plywood end. The dado for the shelves or a raised-panel or Spanish end is 3/16″ deep but it is 3/8″ deep on a 3/4″ thick plywood end.

There are three cabinets that use the raised-panel or Spanish ends—the refrigerator or 12″ high wall cabinet, the 30″ high wall cabinet, and the base cabinet. These ends can be computed from the following tables:

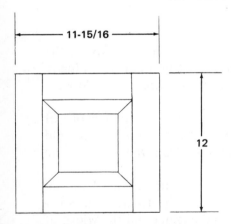

No.	Width (″)	Length (″)	Thickness (″)	Part
2	2-1/4	12	7/8	Stiles
2	2-1/4	8-3/16	7/8	Rails
1	8-3/16	8-1/4	9/16	Panel

Fig. 11-1   Raised-panel refrigerator cabinet end.

No.	Width (″)	Length (″)	Thickness (″)	Part
2	2-1/4	12	7/8	Stiles
2	3-1/4	8-3/16	7/8	Rails
1	8-3/16	8-1/4	1/4	Panel

Fig. 11-2   Spanish refrigerator cabinet end.

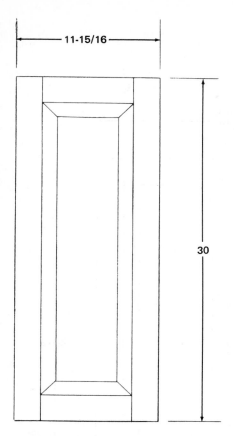

No.	Width (″)	Length (″)	Thickness (″)	Part
2	2-1/4	30	7/8	Stiles
2	2-1/4	8-3/16	7/8	Rails
1	8-3/16	26-1/4	9/16	Panel

Fig. 11-3 Raised-panel 30″ high wall cabinet end.

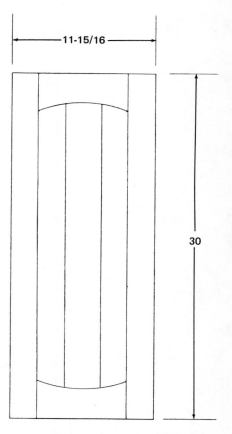

No.	Width (″)	Length (″)	Thickness (″)	Part
2	2-1/4	30	7/8	Stiles
2	3-1/4	8-3/16	7/8	Rails
1	8-3/16	26-1/4	1/4	Panel

Fig. 11-4 Spanish 30″ high wall cabinet end.

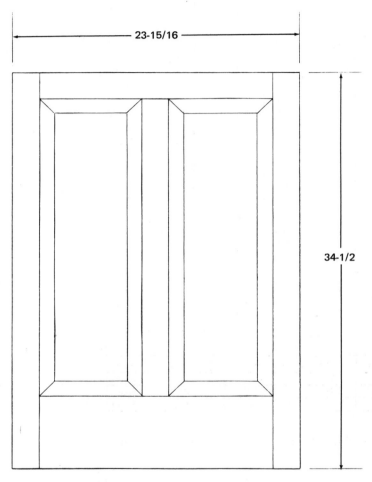

No.	Width ($''$)	Length ($''$)	Thickness ($''$)	Part
2	2-1/4	34-1/2	7/8	Stiles
1	2-1/4	20-3/16	7/8	Top rail
1	6-1/4	20-3/16	7/8	Bottom rail
1	2-1/4	26-3/4	7/8	Mull
2	9-9/32	26-3/4	9/16	Panels

Fig. 11-5   Raised-panel base cabinet end.

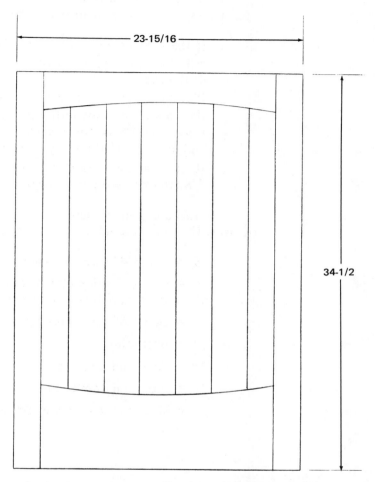

No.	Width (")	Length (")	Thickness (")	Part
2	2-1/4	34-1/2	7/8	Stiles
1	3-1/4	20-3/16	7/8	Top rail
1	7-1/4	20-3/16	7/8	Bottom rail
1	20-3/16	26-3/4	1/4	Panel

Fig. 11-6   Spanish base cabinet end.

There are three different combinations for computing the dimensions of the component parts when the lock joint is used.

1. If the cabinet does not have a finished or exposed end on either end, a 3/4″ thick plywood end is used on each end of the cabinet.
2. If the cabinet has a finished or exposed end on one end of the cabinet and an unfinished end on the other, a 7/8″ thick raised-panel or Spanish end is used on the finished end and a 3/4″ thick plywood end on the unfinished end.
3. If the cabinet has two finished or exposed ends, two 7/8″ thick raised-panel or Spanish ends are used.

All the component parts for all cabinets can be computed by using the following tables and these seven different codes:

a = two 3/4″ thick plywood ends.

b = one 3/4″ thick plywood end and one 7/8″ thick raised-panel or Spanish end.

c = two 7/8″ thick raised-panel or Spanish ends.

* = butt joint.

** = dado and lip joint.

‡ = monorail drawer guide.

\# = side-mounted drawer guide.

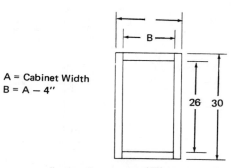

A = Cabinet Width
B = A – 4″

W-1 9″ to 24″ one-door wall cabinet.

No.	Width (″)		Length (″)			Thickness (″)		Part
FACE PLATE								
2	2		30			3/4		Stiles
2	2		A - 2-1/2			3/4		Rails
CABINET WITH BUTT OR DADO & LIP JOINT								
	*	**						
2	11-1/4	11-1/2	30			3/4		Wall Ends
4	11		A - 7/8			3/4		Shelves
1	30		A - 5/8			1/4		Back
CABINET WITH LOCK JOINT								
2	11-15/16		30			3/4 or 7/8		Wall Ends
			a	b	c			
4	11		A - 1-1/16	A - 1-5/16	A - 1-9/16	3/4		Shelves
1	30		A - 3/8	A - 5/8	A - 7/8	1/4		Back
DOOR								
1	B + 5/8		26-5/8			3/4		Plywood Door or
1	B + 5/8		26-5/8			7/8		Raised Panel or Spanish Door
RAISED PANEL OR SPANISH DOOR PARTS								
2	2-1/4		26-5/8			7/8		Stiles
	RP	S						
2	2-1/4	3-1/4	B - 3-1/8			7/8		Rails
						RP	S	
1	B - 3-1/8		22-7/8			9/16	1/4	Panel

* = Butt Joint   a = 2-3/4″ Thick Ends   RP = Raised Panel Door
** = Dado & Lip Joint   b = 1-3/4″ & 1-7/8″ Thick Ends   S = Spanish Door
                       c = 2-7/8″ Thick Ends

145

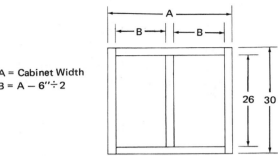

A = Cabinet Width
B = A − 6″ ÷ 2

W-2 24″ to 42″ two-door wall cabinet.

No.	Width ('')		Length ('')			Thickness ('')		Part
FACE PLATE								
2	2		30			3/4		Stiles
2	2		A - 2-1/2			3/4		Rails
1	2		27-1/2			3/4		Mulls
CABINET WITH BUTT OR DADO & LIP JOINT								
2	* 11-1/4	** 11-1/2	30			3/4		Wall Ends
4	11		A - 7/8			3/4		Shelves
1	30		A - 5/8			1/4		Back
CABINET WITH LOCK JOINT								
2	11-15/16		30			3/4 or 7/8		Wall Ends
4	11		a A - 1-1/16	b A - 1-5/16	c A - 1-9/16	3/4		Shelves
1	30		A - 3/8	A - 5/8	A - 7/8	1/4		Back
DOORS								
2	B + 5/8		26-5/8			3/4		Plywood Doors or
2	B + 5/8		26-5/8			7/8		Raised Panel or Spanish Doors
RAISED PANEL OR SPANISH DOOR PARTS								
4	2-1/4		26-5/8			7/8		Stiles
4	RP 2-1/4	S 3-1/4	B - 3-1/8			7/8		Rails
2	B - 3-1/8		22-7/8			RP 9/16	S 1/4	Panels

* = Butt Joint	a = 2-3/4'' Thick Ends	RP = Raised Panel Door
** = Dado & Lip Joint	b = 1-3/4'' & 1-7/8'' Thick Ends	S = Spanish Door
	c = 2-7/8'' Thick Ends	

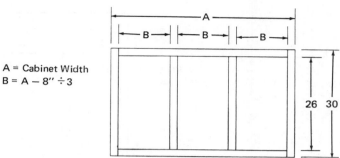

A = Cabinet Width
B = A — 8″ ÷ 3

26 30

W-3 42″ to 60″ three-door wall cabinet.

No.	Width (″)		Length (″)			Thickness (″)		Part
FACE PLATE								
2	2		30			3/4		Stiles
2	2		A - 2-1/2			3/4		Rails
2	2		27-1/2			3/4		Mulls
CABINET WITH BUTT OR DADO & LIP JOINT								
2	* 11-1/4	** 11-1/2	30			3/4		Wall Ends
4	11		A - 7/8			3/4		Shelves
1	30		A - 5/8			1/4		Back
CABINET WITH LOCK JOINT								
2	11-15/16		30			3/4 or 7/8		Wall Ends
4	11		a A - 1-1/16	b A - 1-5/16	c A - 1-9/16	3/4		Shelves
1	30		A - 3/8	A - 5/8	A - 7/8	1/4		Back
DOORS								
3	B + 5/8		26-5/8			3/4		Plywood Doors or
3	B + 5/8		26-5/8			7/8		Raised Panel or Spanish Doors
RAISED PANEL OR SPANISH DOOR PARTS								
6	2-1/4		26-5/8			7/8		Stiles
6	RP 2-1/4	S 3-1/4	B - 3-1/8			7/8		Rails
3	B - 3-1/8		22-7/8			RP 9/16	S 1/4	Panels

* = Butt Joint   a = 2-3/4″ Thick Ends   RP = Raised Panel Door
** = Dado & Lip Joint   b = 1-3/4″ & 1-7/8″ Thick Ends   S = Spanish Door
                                c = 2-7/8″ Thick Ends

147

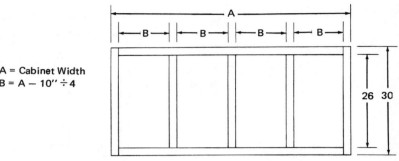

A = Cabinet Width

B = A − 10″ ÷ 4

W-4 60″ to 78″ four-door wall cabinet.

No.	Width ('')		Length ('')			Thickness ('')		Part
FACE PLATE								
2	2		30			3/4		Stiles
2	2		A - 2-1/2			3/4		Rails
3	2		27-1/2			3/4		Mulls
CABINET WITH BUTT OR DADO & LIP JOINT								
	*	**						
2	11-1/4	11-1/2	30			3/4		Wall Ends
4	11		A - 7/8			3/4		Shelves
1	30		A - 5/8			1/4		Back
CABINET WITH LOCK JOINT								
2	11-15/16		30			3/4 or 7/8		Wall Ends
			a	b	c			
4	11		A - 1-1/16	A - 1-5/16	A - 1-9/16	3/4		Shelves
1	30		A - 3/8	A - 5/8	A - 7/8	1/4		Back
DOORS								
4	B + 5/8		26-5/8			3/4		Plywood Doors or
4	B + 5/8		26-5/8			7/8		Raised Panel or Spanish Doors
RAISED PANEL OR SPANISH DOOR PARTS								
8	2-1/4		26-5/8			7/8		Stiles
	RP	S						
8	2-1/4	3-1/4	B - 3-1/8			7/8		Rails
						RP	S	
4	B - 3-1/8		22-7/8			9/16	1/4	Panels

* = Butt Joint   a = 2-3/4'' Thick Ends   RP = Raised Panel Door

** = Dado & Lip Joint   b = 1-3/4'' & 1-7/8'' Thick Ends   S = Spanish Door

                       c = 2-7/8'' Thick Ends

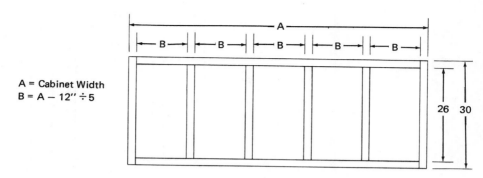

A = Cabinet Width
B = A − 12″ ÷ 5

W-5 78″ to 96″ five-door wall cabinet.

No.	Width (″)		Length (″)			Thickness (″)		Part
FACE PLATE								
2	2		30			3/4		Stiles
2	2		A - 2-1/2			3/4		Rails
4	2		27-1/2			3/4		Mulls
CABINET WITH BUTT OR DADO & LIP JOINT								
2	* 11-1/4	** 11-1/2	30			3/4		Wall Ends
4	11		A - 7/8			3/4		Shelves
1	30		A - 5/8			1/4		Back
CABINET WITH LOCK JOINT								
2	11-15/16		30			3/4 or 7/8		Wall Ends
4	11		a A - 1-1/16	b A - 1-5/16	c A - 1-9/16	3/4		Shelves
1	30		A - 3/8	A - 5/8	A - 7/8	1/4		Back
DOORS								
5	B + 5/8		26-5/8			3/4		Plywood Doors or
5	B + 5/8		26-5/8			7/8		Raised Panel or Spanish Doors
RAISED PANEL OR SPANISH DOOR PARTS								
10	2-1/4		26-5/8			7/8		Stiles
10	RP 2-1/4	S 3-1/4	B - 3-1/8			7/8		Rails
5	B - 3-1/8		22-7/8			RP 9/16	S 1/4	Panels

* = Butt Joint	a = 2-3/4″ Thick Ends	RP = Raised Panel Door
** = Dado & Lip Joint	b = 1-3/4″ & 1-7/8″ Thick Ends	S = Spanish Door
	c = 2-7/8″ Thick Ends	

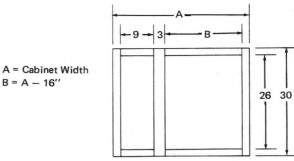

A = Cabinet Width
B = A − 16″

LCW-1 24″ to 36″ one-door left-hand corner wall cabinet.

No.	Width (″)		Length (″)			Thickness (″)		Part
FACE PLATE								
2	2		30			3/4		Stiles
2	2		10-1/2			3/4		Rails
2	2		A - 14-1/2			3/4		Rails
1	3		30			3/4		Mull
CABINET WITH BUTT OR DADO & LIP JOINT								
2	* 11-1/4	** 11-1/2	30			3/4		Wall Ends
4	11		A - 7/8			3/4		Shelves
1	30		A - 5/8			1/4		Back
CABINET WITH LOCK JOINT								
2	11-15/16		30			3/4 or 7/8		Wall Ends
4	11		a A - 1-1/16	b A - 1-5/16	c A - 1-9/16	3/4		Shelves
1	30		A - 3/8	A - 5/8	A - 7/8	1/4		Back
DOOR								
1	B + 5/8		26-5/8			3/4		Plywood Door or
1	B + 5/8		26-5/8			7/8		Raised Panel or Spanish Door
RAISED PANEL OR SPANISH DOOR PARTS								
2	2-1/4		26-5/8			7/8		Stiles
2	RP 2-1/4	S 3-1/4	B - 3-1/8			7/8		Rails
1	B - 3-1/8		22-7/8			RP 9/16	S 1/4	Panel

* = Butt Joint   a = 2-3/4″ Thick Ends   RP = Raised Panel Door
** = Dado & Lip Joint   b = 1-3/4″ & 1-7/8″ Thick Ends   S = Spanish Door
                           c = 2-7/8″ Thick Ends

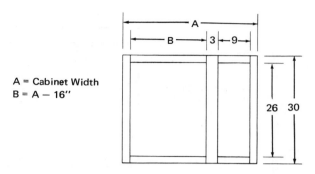

A = Cabinet Width
B = A − 16″

RCW-1 24″ to 36″ one-door right-hand corner wall cabinet.

No.	Width (″)		Length (″)			Thickness (″)		Part
FACE PLATE								
2	2		30			3/4		Stiles
2	2		10-1/2			3/4		Rails
2	2		A - 14-1/2			3/4		Rails
1	3		30			3/4		Mull
CABINET WITH BUTT OR DADO & LIP JOINT								
	*	**						
2	11-1/4	11-1/2	30			3/4		Wall Ends
4	11		A - 7/8			3/4		Shelves
1	30		A - 5/8			1/4		Back
CABINET WITH LOCK JOINT								
2	11-15/16		30			3/4 to 7/8		Wall Ends
			a	b	c			
4	11		A - 1-1/16	A - 1-5/16	A - 1-9/16	3/4		Shelves
1	30		A - 3/8	A - 5/8	A - 7/8	1/4		Back
DOOR								
1	B + 5/8		26-5/8			3/4		Plywood Door or
1	B + 5/8		26-5/8			7/8		Raised Panel or Spanish Door
RAISED PANEL OR SPANISH DOOR PARTS								
2	2-1/4		26-5/8			7/8		Stiles
	RP	S						
2	2-1/4	3-1/4	B - 3-1/8			7/8		Rails
						RP	S	
1	B - 3-1/8		22-7/8			9/16	1/4	Panel

* = Butt Joint   a = 2-3/4″ Thick Ends   RP = Raised Panel Door
** = Dado & Lip Joint   b = 1-3/4″ & 1-7/8″ Thick Ends S = Spanish Door
                         c = 2-7/8″ Thick Ends

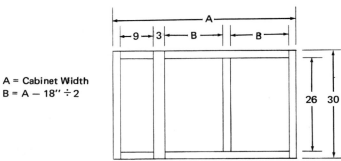

A = Cabinet Width
B = A − 18″ ÷ 2

LCW-2 36″ to 54″ two-door left-hand corner wall cabinet.

No.	Width (″)		Length (″)			Thickness (″)		Part
FACE PLATE								
2	2		30			3/4		Stiles
2	2		10-1/2			3/4		Rails
2	2		A - 14-1/2			3/4		Rails
1	2		27-1/2			3/4		Mulls
1	3		30			3/4		Mull
CABINET WITH BUTT OR DADO & LIP JOINT								
	*	**						
2	11-1/4	11-1/2	30			3/4		Wall Ends
4	11		A - 7/8			3/4		Shelves
1	30		A - 5/8			1/4		Back
CABINET WITH LOCK JOINT								
2	11-15/16		30			3/4 or 7/8		Wall Ends
			a	b	c			
4	11		A - 1-1/16	A - 1-5/16	A - 1-9/16	3/4		Shelves
1	30		A - 3/8	A - 5/8	A - 7/8	1/4		Back
DOORS								
2	B + 5/8		26-5/8			3/4		Plywood Doors or
2	B + 5/8		26-5/8			7/8		Raised Panel or Spanish Doors
RAISED PANEL OR SPANISH DOOR PARTS								
4	2-1/4		26-5/8			7/8		Stiles
	RP	S						
4	2-1/4	3-1/4	B - 3-1/8			7/8		Rails
						RP	S	
2	B - 3-1/8		22-7/8			9/16	1/4	Panels

* = Butt Joint
** = Dado & Lip Joint

a = 2-3/4″ Thick Ends
b = 1-3/4″ & 1-7/8″ Thick Ends
c = 2-7/8″ Thick Ends

RP = Raised Panel Door
S = Spanish Door

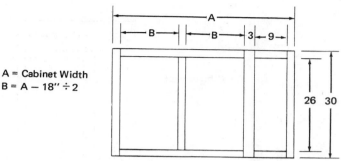

A = Cabinet Width
B = A − 18″ ÷ 2

RCW-2 36″ to 54″ two-door right-hand corner wall cabinet.

No.	Width (″)		Length (″)			Thickness (″)		Part
FACE PLATE								
2	2		30			3/4		Stiles
2	2		10-1/2			3/4		Rails
2	2		A - 14-1/2			3/4		Rails
1	2		27-1/2			3/4		Mulls
1	3		30			3/4		Mull
CABINET WITH BUTT OR DADO & LIP JOINT								
	*	**						
2	11-1/4	11-1/2	30			3/4		Wall Ends
4	11		A - 7/8			3/4		Shelves
1	30		A - 5/8			1/4		Back
CABINET WITH LOCK JOINT								
2	11-15/16		30			3/4 or 7/8		Wall Ends
			a	b	c			
4	11		A - 1-1/16	A - 1-5/16	A - 1-9/16	3/4		Shelves
1	30		A - 3/8	A - 5/8	A - 7/8	1/4		Back
DOORS								
2	B + 5/8		26-5/8			3/4		Plywood Doors or
2	B + 5/8		26-5/8			7/8		Raised Panel or Spanish Doors
RAISED PANEL OR SPANISH DOOR PARTS								
4	2-1/4		26-5/8			7/8		Stiles
	RP	S						
4	2-1/4	3-1/4	B - 3-1/8			7/8		Rails
						RP	S	
2	B - 3-1/8		22-7/8			9/16	1/4	Panels

* = Butt Joint   a = 2-3/4″ Thick Ends   RP = Raised Panel Door
** = Dado & Lip Joint   b = 1-3/4″ & 1-7/8″ Thick Ends   S = Spanish Door
                         c = 2-7/8″ Thick Ends

153

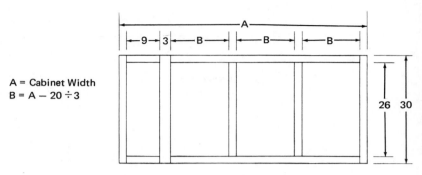

A = Cabinet Width
B = A − 20 ÷ 3

LCW-3 54" to 72" three-door left-hand corner wall cabinet.

No.	Width ('')		Length ('')			Thickness ('')		Part
FACE PLATE								
2	2		30			3/4		Stiles
2	2		10-1/2			3/4		Rails
2	2		A - 14-1/2			3/4		Rails
2	2		27-1/2			3/4		Mulls
1	3		30			3/4		Mull
CABINET WITH BUTT OR DADO & LIP JOINT								
	*	**						
2	11-1/4	11-1/2	30			3/4		Wall Ends
4	11		A - 7/8			3/4		Shelves
1	30		A - 5/8			1/4		Back
CABINET WITH LOCK JOINT								
2	11-15/16		30			3/4 or 7/8		Wall Ends
			a	b	c			
4	11		A - 1-1/16	A - 1-5/16	A - 1-9/16	3/4		Shelves
1	30		A - 3/8	A - 5/8	A - 7/8	1/4		Back
DOORS								
3	B + 5/8		26-5/8			3/4		Plywood Doors or
3	B + 5/8		26-5/8			7/8		Raised Panel or Spanish Doors
RAISED PANEL OR SPANISH DOOR PARTS								
6	2-1/4		26-5/8			7/8		Stiles
	RP	S						
6	2-1/4	3-1/4	B - 3-1/8			7/8		Rails
						RP	S	
3	B - 3-1/8		22-7/8			9/16	1/4	Panels

* = Butt Joint	a = 2-3/4'' Thick Ends	RP = Raised Panel Door
** = Dado & Lip Joint	b = 1-3/4'' & 1-7/8'' Thick Ends	S = Spanish Door
	c = 2-7/8'' Thick Ends	

154

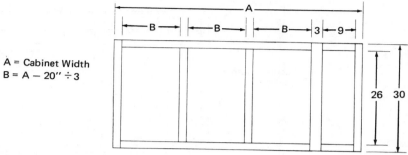

A = Cabinet Width
B = A − 20″ ÷ 3

RCW-3 54″ to 72″ three-door right-hand corner wall cabinet.

No.	Width (″)		Length (″)			Thickness (″)		Part
			FACE PLATE					
2	2		30			3/4		Stiles
2	2		10-1/2			3/4		Rails
2	2		A - 14-1/2			3/4		Rails
2	2		27-1/2			3/4		Mulls
1	3		30			3/4		Mull
			CABINET WITH BUTT OR DADO & LIP JOINT					
	*	**						
2	11-1/4	11-1/2	30			3/4		Wall Ends
4	11		A - 7/8			3/4		Shelves
1	30		A - 5/8			1/4		Back
			CABINET WITH LOCK JOINT					
2	11-15/16		30			3/4 or 7/8		Wall Ends
			a	b	c			
4	11		A - 1-1/16	A - 1-5/16	A - 1-9/16	3/4		Shelves
1	30		A - 3/8	A - 5/8	A - 7/8	1/4		Back
			DOORS					
3	B + 5/8		26-5/8			3/4		Plywood Doors or
3	B + 5/8		26-5/8			7/8		Raised Panel or Spanish Doors
			RAISED PANEL OR SPANISH DOOR PARTS					
6	2-1/4		26-5/8			7/8		Stiles
	RP	S						
6	2-1/4	3-1/4	B - 3-1/8			7/8		Rails
						RP	S	
3	B - 3-1/8		22-7/8			9/16	1/4	Panels

```
 *  = Butt Joint           a = 2-3/4″ Thick Ends        RP = Raised Panel Door
 ** = Dado & Lip Joint      b = 1-3/4″ & 1-7/8″ Thick Ends   S = Spanish Door
                            c = 2-7/8″ Thick Ends
```

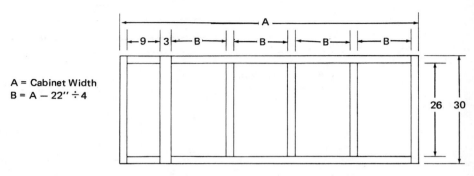

A = Cabinet Width
B = A − 22″ ÷ 4

LCW-4 72″ to 96″ four-door left-hand corner wall cabinet.

No.	Width (″)		Length (″)			Thickness (″)		Part
FACE PLATE								
2	2		30			3/4		Stiles
2	2		10-1/2			3/4		Rails
2	2		A - 14-1/2			3/4		Rails
3	2		27-1/2			3/4		Mulls
1	3		30			3/4		Mull
CABINET WITH BUTT OR DADO & LIP JOINT								
2	* 11-1/4	** 11-1/2	30			3/4		Wall Ends
4	11		A - 7/8			3/4		Shelves
1	30		A - 5/8			1/4		Back
CABINET WITH LOCK JOINT								
2	11-15/16		30			3/4 or 7/8		Wall Ends
4	11		a A - 1-1/16	b A - 1-5/16	c A - 1-9/16	3/4		Shelves
1	30		a A - 3/8	b A - 5/8	c A - 7/8	1/4		Back
DOORS								
4	B + 5/8		26-5/8			3/4		Plywood Doors or
4	B + 5/8		26-5/8			7/8		Raised Panel or Spanish Doors
RAISED PANEL OR SPANISH DOOR PARTS								
8	2-1/4		26-5/8			7/8		Stiles
8	RP 2-1/4	S 3-1/4	B - 3-1/8			7/8		Rails
4	B - 3-1/8		22-7/8			RP 9/16	S 1/4	Panels

```
  *  = Butt Joint            a = 2-3/4″ Thick Ends          RP = Raised Panel Door
 **  = Dado & Lip Joint      b = 1-3/4″ & 1-7/8″ Thick Ends  S = Spanish Door
                             c = 2-7/8″ Thick Ends
```

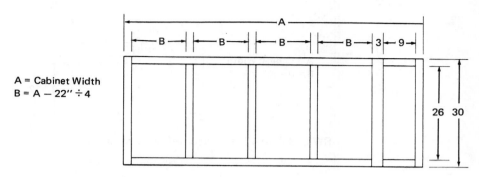

A = Cabinet Width
B = A − 22″ ÷ 4

RCW-4 72″ to 96″ four-door right-hand corner wall cabinet.

No.	Width (″)		Length (″)			Thickness (″)		Part
FACE PLATE								
2	2		30			3/4		Stiles
2	2		10-1/2			3/4		Rails
2	2		A - 14-1/2			3/4		Rails
3	2		27-1/2			3/4		Mulls
1	3		30			3/4		Mull
CABINET WITH BUTT OR DADO & LIP JOINT								
	*	**						
2	11-1/4	11-1/2	30			3/4		Wall Ends
4	11		A - 7/8			3/4		Shelves
1	30		A - 5/8			1/4		Back
CABINET WITH LOCK JOINT								
2	11-15/16		30			3/4 or 7/8		Wall Ends
			a	b	c			
4	11		A - 1-1/16	A - 1-5/16	A - 1-9/16	3/4		Shelves
1	30		A - 3/8	A - 5/8	A - 7/8	1/4		Back
DOORS								
4	B + 5/8		26-5/8			3/4		Plywood Doors or
4	B + 5/8		26-5/8			7/8		Raised Panel or Spanish Doors
RAISED PANEL OR SPANISH DOOR PARTS								
8	2-1/4		26-5/8			7/8		Stiles
	RP	S						
8	2-1/4	3-1/4	B - 3-1/8			7/8		Rails
						RP	S	
4	B - 3-1/8		22-7/8			9/16	1/4	Panels

* = Butt Joint   a = 2-3/4″ Thick Ends   RP = Raised Panel Door
** = Dado & Lip Joint   b = 1-3/4″ & 1-7/8″ Thick Ends   S = Spanish Door
                 c = 2-7/8″ Thick Ends

157

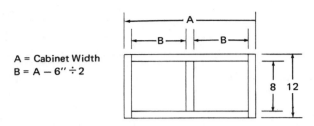

A = Cabinet Width
B = A − 6″ ÷ 2

RW-2 30″ to 42″ two-door refrigerator cabinet.

No.	Width ('')		Length ('')			Thickness ('')		Part
FACE PLATE								
2	2		12			3/4		Stiles
2	2		A - 2-1/2			3/4		Rails
1	2		9-1/2			3/4		Mulls
CABINET WITH BUTT OR DADO & LIP JOINT								
	*	**						
2	11-1/4	11-1/2	12			3/4		Wall Ends
2	11		A - 7/8			3/4		Shelves
1	12		A - 5/8			1/4		Back
CABINET WITH LOCK JOINT								
2	11-15/16		12			3/4 or 7/8		Wall Ends
			a	b	c			
2	11		A - 1-1/16	A - 1-5/16	A - 1-9/16	3/4		Shelves
1	12		A - 3/8	A - 5/8	A - 7/8	1/4		Back
DOORS								
2	B + 5/8		8-5/8			3/4		Plywood Doors or
2	B + 5/8		8-5/8			7/8		Raised Panel or Spanish Doors
RAISED PANEL OR SPANISH DOOR PARTS								
4	2-1/4		8-5/8			7/8		Stiles
	RP	S						
4	2-1/4	3-1/4	B - 3-1/8			7/8		Rails
						RP	S	
2	B - 3-1/8		4-7/8			9/16	1/4	Panels

* = Butt Joint
** = Dado & Lip Joint

a = 2-3/4″ Thick Ends
b = 1-3/4″ & 1-7/8″ Thick Ends
c = 2-7/8″ Thick Ends

RP = Raised Panel Door
S = Spanish Door

158

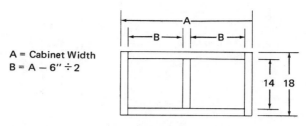

A = Cabinet Width
B = A − 6″ ÷ 2

VW-2 30″ to 42″ two-door Vent-A-Hood cabinet.

No.	Width (″)		Length (″)			Thickness (″)		Part
FACE PLATE								
2	2		18			3/4		Stiles
2	2		A - 2-1/2			3/4		Rails
1	2		15-1/2			3/4		Mulls
CABINET WITH BUTT OR DADO & LIP JOINT								
2	* 11-1/4	** 11-1/2	18			3/4		Wall Ends
2	11		A - 7/8			3/4		Shelves
1	18		A - 5/8			1/4		Back
CABINET WITH LOCK JOINT								
2	11-15/16		18			3/4 or 7/8		Wall Ends
2	11		a A - 1-1/16	b A - 1-5/16	c A - 1-9/16	3/4		Shelves
1	18		A - 3/8	A - 5/8	A - 7/8	1/4		Back
DOORS								
2	B + 5/8		14-5/8			3/4		Plywood Doors or
2	B + 5/8		14-5/8			7/8		Raised Panel or Spanish Doors
RAISED PANEL OR SPANISH DOOR PARTS								
4	2-1/4		14-5/8			7/8		Stiles
4	RP 2-1/4	S 3-1/4	B - 3-1/8			7/8		Rails
2	B - 3-1/8		10-7/8			RP 9/16	S 1/4	Panels

* = Butt Joint
** = Dado & Lip Joint

a = 2-3/4″ Thick Ends
b = 1-3/4″ & 1-7/8″ Thick Ends
c = 2-7/8″ Thick Ends

RP = Raised Panel Door
S = Spanish Door

159

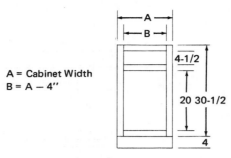

A = Cabinet Width
B = A − 4″

B-1 9″ to 24″ one-door base cabinet.

No.	Width (″)		Length (″)			Thickness (″)		Part
FACE PLATE								
2	2		30-1/2			3/4		Stiles
3	2		A - 2-1/2			3/4		Rails
CABINET WITH BUTT OR DADO & LIP JOINT								
	*	**						
2	23-1/4	23-1/2	34-1/2			3/4		Base Ends
1	23		A - 7/8			3/4		Bottom
1	23-7/8		A - 5/8			1/4		Back
1	7		A - 1-5/8			3/4		Nailing Strip
1	4		A			3/4		Toe Board
CABINET WITH LOCK JOINT								
2	23-15/16		34-1/2			3/4 or 7/8		Base Ends
			a	b	c			
1	23		A - 1-1/16	A - 1-5/16	A - 1-9/16	3/4		Bottom
1	23-7/8		A-3/8	A - 5/8	A - 7/8	1/4		Back
1	7		A - 1-13/16			3/4		Nailing Strip
1	4		A			3/4		Toe Board
DOOR								
1	B + 5/8		20-5/8			3/4		Plywood Door or
1	B + 5/8		20-5/8			7/8		Raised Panel or Spanish Door
RAISED PANEL OR SPANISH DOOR PARTS								
2	2-1/4		20-5/8			7/8		Stiles
	RP	S						
2	2-1/4	3-1/4	B - 3-1/8			7/8		Rails
						RP	S	
1	B - 3-1/8		16-7/8			9/16	1/4	Panel
DRAWER								
1	5-1/8		B + 5/8			3/4		Drawer Front
			‡		#			
2	4-1/8		B - 1/4		B - 1-1/16	1/2		Front & Back Ends
2	4-1/8		18			1/2		Drawer Sides
	‡	#						
1	B - 3/4	B - 1-9/16	17-5/8			1/4		Plywood Bottom

* = Butt Joint	b = 1-3/4″ & 1-7/8″ Thick Ends	# = Side Mount Drawer Slide
** = Dado & Lip Joint	c = 2-7/8″ Thick Ends	RP = Raised Panel Door
a = 2-3/4″ Thick Ends	‡ = Monorail Drawer Slide	S = Spanish Door

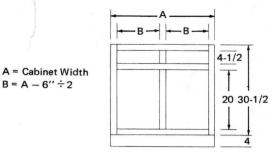

A = Cabinet Width
B = A − 6″ ÷ 2

B-2 24″ to 42″ two-door base cabinet.

No.	Width (″)			Length (″)			Thickness (″)		Part
FACE PLATE									
2	2			30-1/2			3/4		Stiles
3	2			A - 2-1/2			3/4		Rails
1	2			21-1/2			3/4		Mulls
1	2			6			3/4		Mulls
CABINET WITH BUTT OR DADO & LIP JOINT									
	*	**							
2	23-1/4	23-1/2		34-1/2			3/4		Base Ends
1	23			A - 7/8			3/4		Bottom
1	23-7/8			A - 5/8			1/4		Back
1	7			A - 1-5/8			3/4		Nailing Strip
1	4			A			3/4		Toe Board
CABINET WITH LOCK JOINT									
2	23-15/16			34-1/2			3/4 or 7/8		Base Ends
			a	b	c				
1	23		A - 1-1/16	A - 1-5/16	A - 1-9/16		3/4		Bottom
1	23-7/8		A - 3/8	A - 5/8	A - 7/8		1/4		Back
1	7		A - 1-13/16				3/4		Nailing Strip
1	4		A				3/4		Toe Board
DOORS									
2	B + 5/8			20-5/8			3/4		Plywood Doors or
2	B + 5/8			20-5/8			7/8		Raised Panel or Spanish Doors
RAISED PANEL OR SPANISH DOOR PARTS									
4	2-1/4			20-5/8			7/8		Stiles
	RP	S							
4	2-1/4	3-1/4		B - 3-1/8			7/8		Rails
							RP	S	
2	B - 3-1/8			16-7/8			9/16	1/4	Panels
DRAWERS									
2	5-1/8			B + 5/8			3/4		Drawer Fronts
			‡	#					
4	4-1/8		B - 1/4	B - 1-1/16			1/2		Front & Back Ends
4	4-1/8			18			1/2		Drawer Sides
	‡	#							
2	B - 3/4	B - 1-9/16		17-5/8			1/4		Plywood Bottoms

* = Butt Joint	b = 1-3/4″ & 1-7/8″ Thick Ends	# = Side Mount Drawer Slide
** = Dado & Lip Joint	c = 2-7/8″ Thick Ends	RP = Raised Panel Door
a = 2-3/4″ Thick Ends	‡ = Monorail Drawer Slide	S = Spanish Door

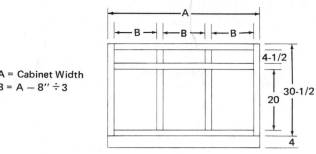

A = Cabinet Width
B = A − 8″ ÷ 3

B-3 42″ to 60″ three-door base cabinet.

No.	Width (″)		Length (″)			Thickness (″)		Part
FACE PLATE								
2	2		30-1/2			3/4		Stiles
3	2		A - 2-1/2			3/4		Rails
2	2		21-1/2			3/4		Mulls
2	2		6			3/4		Mulls
CABINET WITH BUTT OR DADO & LIP JOINT								
	*	**						
2	23-1/4	23-1/2	34-1/2			3/4		Base Ends
1	23		A - 7/8			3/4		Bottom
1	23-7/8		A - 5/8			1/4		Back
1	7		A - 1-5/8			3/4		Nailing Strip
1	4		A			3/4		Toe Board
CABINET WITH LOCK JOINT								
2	23-15/16		34-1/2			3/4 or 7/8		Base Ends
			a	b	c			
1	23		A - 1-1/16	A - 1-5/16	A - 1-9/16	3/4		Bottom
1	23-7/8		A - 3/8	A - 5/8	A - 7/8	1/4		Back
1	7		A - 1-13/16			3/4		Nailing Strip
1	4		A			3/4		Toe Board
DOORS								
3	B + 5/8		20-5/8			3/4		Plywood Doors or
3	B + 5/8		20-5/8			7/8		Raised Panel or Spanish Doors
RAISED PANEL OR SPANISH DOOR PARTS								
6	2-1/4		20-5/8			7/8		Stiles
	RP	S						
6	2-1/4	3-1/4	B - 3-1/8			7/8		Rails
						RP	S	
3	B - 3-1/8		16-7/8			9/16	1/4	Panels
DRAWERS								
3	5-1/8		B + 5/8			3/4		Drawer Fronts
			‡	#				
6	4-1/8		B - 1/4	B - 1-1/16		1/2		Front & Back Ends
6	4-1/8		18			1/2		Drawer Sides
	‡	#						
3	B - 3/4	B - 1-9/16	17-5/8			1/4		Plywood Bottoms

   * = Butt Joint   b = 1-3/4″ & 1-7/8″ Thick Ends   # = Side Mount Drawer Slide
  ** = Dado & Lip Joint   c = 2-7/8″ Thick Ends   RP = Raised Panel Door
   a = 2-3/4″ Thick Ends   ‡ = Monorail Drawer Slide   S = Spanish Door

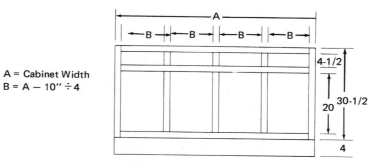

A = Cabinet Width
B = A − 10″ ÷ 4

B-4 60″ to 78″ four-door base cabinet.

FACE PLATE

No.	Width (″)	Length (″)	Thickness (″)	Part
2	2	30-1/2	3/4	Stiles
3	2	A - 2-1/2	3/4	Rails
3	2	21-1/2	3/4	Mulls
3	2	6	3/4	Mulls

CABINET WITH BUTT OR DADO & LIP JOINT

No.	Width (″) *	Width (″) **	Length (″)	Thickness (″)	Part
2	23-1/4	23-1/2	34-1/2	3/4	Base Ends
1	23		A - 7/8	3/4	Bottom
1	23-7/8		A - 5/8	1/4	Back
1	7		A - 1-5/8	3/4	Nailing Strip
1	4		A	3/4	Toe Board

CABINET WITH LOCK JOINT

No.	Width (″)	Length (″) a	Length (″) b	Length (″) c	Thickness (″)	Part
2	23-15/16	34-1/2			3/4 or 7/8	Base Ends
1	23	A - 1-1/16	A - 1-5/16	A - 1-9/16	3/4	Bottom
1	23-7/8	A - 3/8	A - 5/8	A - 7/8	1/4	Back
1	7	A - 1-13/16			3/4	Nailing Strip
1	4	A			3/4	Toe Board

DOORS

No.	Width (″)	Length (″)	Thickness (″)	Part
4	B + 5/8	20-5/8	3/4	Plywood Doors or
4	B + 5/8	20-5/8	7/8	Raised Panel or Spanish Doors

RAISED PANEL OR SPANISH DOOR PARTS

No.	Width (″)		Length (″)	Thickness (″)		Part
8	2-1/4		20-5/8	7/8		Stiles
8	RP 2-1/4	S 3-1/4	B - 3-1/8	7/8		Rails
4	B - 3-1/8		16-7/8	RP 9/16	S 1/4	Panels

DRAWERS

No.	Width (″)		Length (″) ‡	Length (″) #	Thickness (″)	Part
4	5-1/8		B + 5/8		3/4	Drawer Fronts
8	4-1/8		B - 1/4	B - 1-1/16	1/2	Front & Back Ends
8	4-1/8		18		1/2	Drawer Sides
4	B - 3/4 ‡	B - 1-9/16 #	17-5/8		1/4	Plywood Bottoms

* = Butt Joint   b = 1-3/4″ & 1-7/8″ Thick Ends   # = Side Mount Drawer Slide
** = Dado & Lip Joint   c = 2-7/8″ Thick Ends   RP = Raised Panel Door
a = 2-3/4″ Thick Ends   ‡ = Monorail Drawer Slide   S = Spanish Door

163

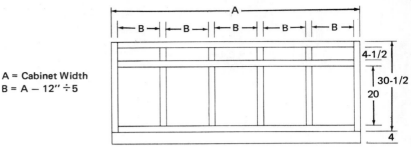

A = Cabinet Width
B = A − 12″ ÷ 5

B-5 78″ to 96″ five-door base cabinet.

No.	Width (″)		Length (″)			Thickness (″)		Part
FACE PLATE								
2	2		30-1/2			3/4		Stiles
3	2		A - 2-1/2			3/4		Rails
4	2		21-1/2			3/4		Mulls
4	2		6			3/4		Mulls
CABINET WITH BUTT OR DADO & LIP JOINT								
	*	**						
2	23-1/4	23-1/2	34-1/2			3/4		Base Ends
1	23		A - 7/8			3/4		Bottom
1	23-7/8		A - 5/8			1/4		Back
1	7		A - 1-5/8			3/4		Nailing Strip
1	4		A			3/4		Toe Board
CABINET WITH LOCK JOINT								
2	23-15/16		34-1/2			3/4 or 7/8		Base Ends
			a	b	c			
1	23		A - 1-1/16	A - 1-5/16	A - 1-9/16	3/4		Bottom
1	23-7/8		A - 3/8	A - 5/8	A - 7/8	1/4		Back
1	7		A - 1-13/16			3/4		Nailing Strip
1	4		A			3/4		Toe Board
DOORS								
5	B + 5/8		20-5/8			3/4		Plywood Doors or
5	B + 5/8		20-5/8			7/8		Raised Panel or Spanish Doors
RAISED PANEL OR SPANISH DOOR PARTS								
10	2-1/4		20-5/8			7/8		Stiles
	RP	S						
10	2-1/4	3-1/4	B - 3-1/8			7/8		Rails
						RP	S	
5	B - 3-1/8		16-7/8			9/16	1/4	Panels
DRAWERS								
5	5-1/8		B + 5/8			3/4		Drawer Fronts
			‡	#				
10	4-1/8		B - 1/4	B - 1-1/16		1/2		Front & Back Ends
10	4-1/8		18			1/2		Drawer Sides
	‡	#						
5	B - 3/4	B - 1-9/16	17-5/8			1/4		Plywood Bottoms

* = Butt Joint   b = 1-3/4″ & 1-7/8″ Thick Ends   # = Side Mount Drawer Slide
** = Dado & Lip Joint   c = 2-7/8″ Thick Ends   RP = Raised Panel Door
a = 2-3/4″ Thick Ends   ‡ = Monorail Drawer Slide   S = Spanish Door

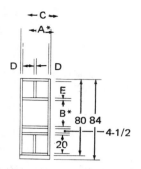

*A & B dimensions are determined by the manufacturers specifications.

A = Oven Width
B = Oven Height
C = A + 4"
D = C − 6" ÷ 2
E = 84" − (B + 38-1/2"

Four-door one-drawer oven cabinet.

No.	Width (")		Length (")		Thickness (")		Part
FACE PLATE							
2	2		80		3/4		Stiles
5	2		A + 1-1/2		3/4		Rails
1	2		E + 1-1/2		3/4		Mull
1	2		21-1/2		3/4		Mull
CABINET WITH BUTT OR DADO & LIP JOINT							
	*	**					
2	24-1/2	24-1/2	84		3/4		Oven Ends
3	24		C - 7/8		3/4		Shelves
1	C - 5/8		78-13/16		1/4		Back
1	4		C		3/4		Toe Board
CABINET WITH LOCK JOINT							
2	24-15/16		84		3/4 or 7/8		Oven Ends
3	24		a C - 1-1/16	b C - 1-5/16	c C - 1-9/16	3/4	Bottom
1	a C - 3/8	b C - 5/8	c C - 7/8	78-13/16		1/4	Back
1	4		C		3/4		Toe Board
DOORS							
2	D + 5/8		E + 5/8		3/4		Plywood Doors
2	D + 5/8		20-5/8		3/4		Plywood Doors or
2	D + 5/8		E + 5/8		7/8		Raised Panel or
2	D + 5/8		20-5/8		7/8		Spanish Doors
RAISED PANEL OR SPANISH DOOR PARTS							
4	2-1/4		E + 5/8		7/8		Stiles
4	2-1/4		20-5/8		7/8		Stiles
8	RP 2-1/4	S 3-1/4	D + 5/8		7/8		Rails
2	D - 3-1/8		E - 3-1/8		RP 9/16	S 1/4	Panels
2	D - 3-1/8		16-7/8		9/16	1/4	Panels
DRAWER							
1	5-1/8		A + 5/8		3/4		Drawer Front
2	4-1/8		‡ A - 1/4	# A - 1-1/16	1/2		Front & Back Ends
2	4-1/8		18		1/2		Drawer Sides
1	‡ A - 3/4	# A - 1-9/16	17-5/8		1/4		Plywood Bottom

* = Butt Joint	b = 1-3/4" & 1-7/8" Thick Ends	# = Side Mount Drawer Slide
** = Dado & Lip Joint	c = 2-7/8" Thick Ends	RP = Raised Panel Door
a = 2-3/4" Thick Ends	‡ = Monorail Drawer Slide	S = Spanish Door

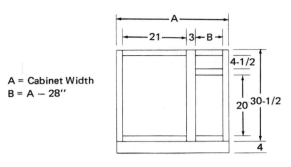

A = Cabinet Width
B = A − 28″

LCB-1 36″ to 48″ one-door left-hand corner base cabinet.

No.	Width (″)			Length (″)			Thickness (″)		Part
				FACE PLATE					
2	2			30-1/2			3/4		Stiles
2	2			22-1/2			3/4		Rails
3	2			A - 26-1/2			3/4		Rails
1	3			30-1/2			3/4		Mull
				CABINET WITH BUTT OR DADO & LIP JOINT					
	*	**							
2	23-1/4	23-1/2		34-1/2			3/4		Base Ends
1	23			A - 7/8			3/4		Bottom
1	23-7/8			A - 5/8			1/4		Back
1	7			A - 1-5/8			3/4		Nailing Strip
1	4			A			3/4		Toe Board
				CABINET WITH LOCK JOINT					
2	23-15/16			34-1/2			3/4 or 7/8		Base Ends
			a	b	c				
1	23		A - 1-1/16	A - 1-5/16	A - 1-9/16		3/4		Bottom
1	23-7/8		A - 3/8	A - 5/8	A - 7/8		1/4		Back
1	7		A - 1-13/16				3/4		Nailing Strip
1	4		A				3/4		Toe Board
				DOOR					
1	B + 5/8			20-5/8			3/4		Plywood Door or
1	B + 5/8			20-5/8			7/8		Raised Panel or Spanish Door
				RAISED PANEL OR SPANISH DOOR PARTS					
2	2-1/4			20-5/8			7/8		Stiles
	RP	S					7/8		
2	2-1/4	3-1/4		B - 3-1/8					Rails
							RP	S	
1	B - 3-1/8			16-7/8			9/16	1/4	Panel
				DRAWER					
1	5-1/8			B + 5/8			3/4		Drawer Front
			‡		#				
2	4-1/8		B - 1/4		B - 1-1/16		1/2		Front & Back Ends
2	4-1/8			18			1/2		Drawer Sides
	‡	#							
1	B - 3/4	B - 1-9/16		17-5/8			1/4		Plywood Bottom

* = Butt Joint	b = 1-3/4″ & 1-7/8″ Thick Ends	# = Side Mount Drawer Slide
** = Dado & Lip Joint	c = 2-7/8″ Thick Ends	RP = Raised Panel Door
a = 2-3/4″ Thick Ends	‡ = Monorail Drawer Slide	S = Spanish Door

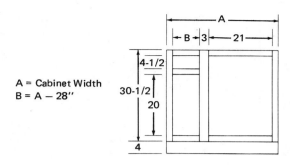

A = Cabinet Width
B = A — 28"

RCB-1 36" to 48" one-door right-hand corner base cabinet.

No.	Width (")		Length (")			Thickness (")		Part
FACE PLATE								
2	2		30-1/2			3/4		Stiles
2	2		22-1/2			3/4		Rails
3	2		A - 26-1/2			3/4		Rails
1	3		30-1/2			3/4		Mull
CABINET WITH BUTT OR DADO & LIP JOINT								
2	* 23-1/4	** 23-1/2	34-1/2			3/4		Base Ends
1	23		A - 7/8			3/4		Bottom
1	23-7/8		A - 5/8			1/4		Back
1	7		A - 1-5/8			3/4		Nailing Strip
1	4		A			3/4		Toe Board
CABINET WITH LOCK JOINT								
2	23-15/16		34-1/2			3/4 or 7/8		Base Ends
1	23		a A - 1-1/16	b A - 1-5/16	c A - 1-9/16	3/4		Bottom
1	23-7/8		A - 3/8	A - 5/8	A - 7/8	1/4		Back
1	7		A - 1-13/16			3/4		Nailing Strip
1	4		A			3/4		Toe Board
DOOR								
1	B + 5/8		20-5/8			3/4		Plywood Door or
1	B + 5/8		20-5/8			7/8		Raised Panel or Spanish Door
RAISED PANEL OR SPANISH DOOR PARTS								
2	2-1/4		20-5/8			7/8		Stiles
2	RP 2-1/4	S 3-1/4	B - 3-1/8			7/8		Rails
1	B - 3-1/8		16-7/8			RP 9/16	S 1/4	Panel
DRAWER								
1	5-1/8		B + 5/8			3/4		Drawer Front
2	4-1/8		‡ B - 1/4	# B - 1-1/16		1/2		Front & Back Ends
2	4-1/8		18			1/2		Drawer Sides
1	‡ B - 3/4	# B - 1-9/16	17-5/8			1/4		Plywood Bottom

* = Butt Joint   b = 1-3/4" & 1-7/8" Thick Ends   # = Side Mount Drawer Slide
** = Dado & Lip Joint   c = 2-7/8" Thick Ends   RP = Raised Panel Door
a = 2-3/4" Thick Ends   ‡ = Monorail Drawer Slide   S = Spanish Door

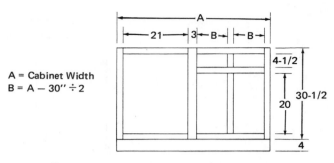

A = Cabinet Width
B = A — 30'' ÷ 2

LCB-2 48" to 66" two-door left-hand corner base cabinet.

No.	Width ('')		Length ('')			Thickness ('')		Part
FACE PLATE								
2	2		30-1/2			3/4		Stiles
2	2		22-1/2			3/4		Rails
3	2		A - 26-1/2			3/4		Rails
1	2		21-1/2			3/4		Mulls
1	2		6			3/4		Mulls
1	3		30-1/2			3/4		Mull
CABINET WITH BUTT OR DADO & LIP JOINT								
	*	**						
2	23-1/4	23-1/2	34-1/2			3/4		Base Ends
1	23		A - 7/8			3/4		Bottom
1	23-7/8		A - 5/8			1/4		Back
1	7		A - 1-5/8			3/4		Nailing Strip
1	4		A			3/4		Toe Board
CABINET WITH LOCK JOINT								
2	23-15/16		34-1/2			3/4 or 7/8		Base Ends
			a	b	c			
1	23		A - 1-1/16	A - 1-5/16	A - 1-9/16	3/4		Bottom
1	23-7/8		A - 3/8	A - 5/8	A - 7/8	1/4		Back
1	7		A - 1-13/16			3/4		Nailing Strip
1	4		A			3/4		Toe Board
DOORS								
2	B + 5/8		20-5/8			3/4		Plywood Doors or
2	B + 5/8		20-5/8			7/8		Raised Panel or Spanish Doors
RAISED PANEL OR SPANISH DOOR PARTS								
4	2-1/4		20-5/8			7/8		Stiles
	RP	S						
4	2-1/4	3-1/4	B - 3-1/8			7/8		Rails
						RP	S	
2	B - 3-1/8		16-7/8			9/16	1/4	Panels
DRAWERS								
2	5-1/8		B + 5/8			3/4		Drawer Fronts
			‡	#				
4	4-1/8		B - 1/4	B - 1-1/16		1/2		Front & Back Ends
4	4-1/8		18			1/2		Drawer Sides
	‡	#						
2	B - 3/4	B - 1-9/16	17-5/8			1/4		Plywood Bottoms

* = Butt Joint
** = Dado & Lip Joint
a = 2-3/4'' Thick Ends
b = 1-3/4'' & 1-7/8'' Thick Ends
c = 2-7/8'' Thick Ends
‡ = Monorail Drawer Slide
# = Side Mount Drawer Slide
RP = Raised Panel Door
S = Spanish Door

168

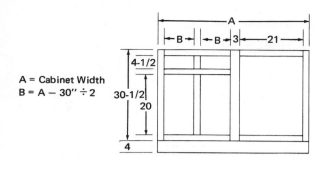

A = Cabinet Width
B = A − 30″ ÷ 2

RCB-2 48″ to 66″ two-door right-hand corner base cabinet.

No.	Width (″)		Length (″)			Thickness (″)		Part
FACE PLATE								
2	2		30-1/2			3/4		Stiles
2	2		22-1/2			3/4		Rails
3	2		A - 26-1/2			3/4		Rails
1	2		21-1/2			3/4		Mulls
1	2		6			3/4		Mulls
1	3		30-1/2			3/4		Mull
CABINET WITH BUTT OR DADO & LIP JOINT								
	*	**						
2	23-1/4	23-1/2	34-1/2			3/4		Base Ends
1	23		A - 7/8			3/4		Bottom
1	23-7/8		A - 5/8			1/4		Back
1	7		A - 1-5/8			3/4		Nailing Strip
1	4		A			3/4		Toe Board
CABINET WITH LOCK JOINT								
2	23-15/16		34-1/2			3/4 or 7/8		Base Ends
			a	b	c			
1	23		A - 1-1/16	A - 1-5/16	A - 1-9/16	3/4		Bottom
1	23-7/8		A - 3/8	A - 5/8	A - 7/8	1/4		Back
1	7		A - 1-13/16			3/4		Nailing Strip
1	4		A			3/4		Toe Board
DOORS								
2	B + 5/8		20-5/8			3/4		Plywood Doors or
2	B + 5/8		20-5/8			7/8		Raised Panel or Spanish Doors
RAISED PANEL OR SPANISH DOOR PARTS								
4	2-1/4		20-5/8			7/8		Stiles
	RP	S						
4	2-1/4	3-1/4	B - 3-1/8			7/8		Rails
						RP	S	
2	B - 3-1/8		16-7/8			9/16	1/4	Panels
DRAWERS								
2	5-1/8		B + 5/8			3/4		Drawer Fronts
			‡	#				
4	4-1/8		B - 1/4	B - 1-1/16		1/2		Front & Back Ends
4	4-1/8		18			1/2		Drawer Sides
	‡	#						
2	B - 3/4	B - 1-9/16	17-5/8			1/4		Plywood Bottoms

* = Butt Joint   b = 1-3/4″ & 1-7/8″ Thick Ends   # = Side Mount Drawer Slide
** = Dado & Lip Joint   c = 2-7/8″ Thick Ends   RP = Raised Panel Door
a = 2-3/4″ Thick Ends   ‡ = Monorail Drawer Slide   S = Spanish Door

169

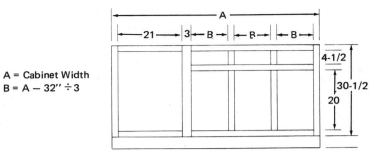

A = Cabinet Width
B = A − 32″ ÷ 3

LCB-3 66″ to 84″ three-door left-hand corner base cabinet.

No.	Width (″)		Length (″)			Thickness (″)		Part
FACE PLATE								
2	2		30-1/2			3/4		Stiles
2	2		22-1/2			3/4		Rails
3	2		A - 26-1/2			3/4		Rails
2	2		21-1/2			3/4		Mulls
2	2		6			3/4		Mulls
1	3		30-1/2			3/4		Mull
CABINET WITH BUTT OR DADO & LIP JOINT								
	*	**						
2	23-1/4	23-1/2	34-1/2			3/4		Base Ends
1	23		A - 7/8			3/4		Bottom
1	23-7/8		A - 5/8			1/4		Back
1	7		A - 1-5/8			3/4		Nailing Strip
1	4		A			3/4		Toe Board
CABINET WITH LOCK JOINT								
2	23-15/16		34-1/2			3/4 or 7/8		Base Ends
			a	b	c			
1	23		A - 1-1/16	A - 1-5/16	A - 1-9/16	3/4		Bottom
1	23-7/8		A - 3/8	A - 5/8	A - 7/8	1/4		Back
1	7		A - 1-13/16			3/4		Nailing Strip
1	4		A			3/4		Toe Board
DOORS								
3	B + 5/8		20-5/8			3/4		Plywood Doors or
3	B + 5/8		20-5/8			7/8		Raised Panel or Spanish Doors
RAISED PANEL OR SPANISH DOOR PARTS								
6	2-1/4		20-5/8			7/8		Stiles
	RP	S						
6	2-1/4	3-1/4	B - 3-1/8			7/8		Rails
						RP	S	
3	B - 3-1/8		16-7/8			9/16	1/4	Panels
DRAWERS								
3	5-1/8		B + 5/8			3/4		Drawer Fronts
			‡	#				
6	4-1/8		B - 1/4	B - 1-1/16		1/2		Front & Back Ends
6	4-1/8		18			1/2		Drawer Sides
	‡	#						
3	B - 3/4	B - 1-9/16	17-5/8			1/4		Plywood Bottoms

* = Butt Joint	b = 1-3/4″ & 1-7/8″ Thick Ends	# = Side Mount Drawer Slide
** = Dado & Lip Joint	c = 2-7/8″ Thick Ends	RP = Raised Panel Door
a = 2-3/4″ Thick Ends	‡ = Monorail Drawer Slide	S = Spanish Door

170

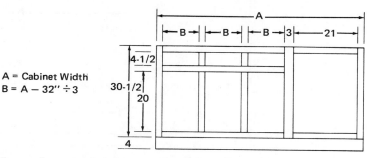

A = Cabinet Width
B = A − 32″ ÷ 3

RCB-3 66″ to 84″ three-door right-hand corner base cabinet.

No.	Width (″)		Length (″)			Thickness (″)		Part
FACE PLATE								
2	2		30-1/2			3/4		Stiles
2	2		22-1/2			3/4		Rails
3	2		A - 26-1/2			3/4		Rails
2	2		21-1/2			3/4		Mulls
2	2		6			3/4		Mulls
1	3		30-1/2			3/4		Mull
CABINET WITH BUTT OR DADO & LIP JOINT								
2	* 23-1/4	** 23-1/2	34-1/2			3/4		Base Ends
1	23		A - 7/8			3/4		Bottom
1	23-7/8		A - 5/8			1/4		Back
1	7		A - 1-5/8			3/4		Nailing Strip
1	4		A			3/4		Toe Board
CABINET WITH LOCK JOINT								
2	23-15/16		34-1/2			3/4 or 7/8		Base Ends
1	23		a A - 1-1/16	b A - 1-5/16	c A - 1-9/16	3/4		Bottom
1	23-7/8		A - 3/8	A - 5/8	A - 7/8	1/4		Back
1	7		A - 1-13/16			3/4		Nailing Strip
1	4		A			3/4		Toe Board
DOORS								
3	B + 5/8		20-5/8			3/4		Plywood Doors or
3	B + 5/8		20-5/8			7/8		Raised Panel or Spanish Doors
RAISED PANEL OR SPANISH DOOR PARTS								
6	2-1/4		20-5/8			7/8		Stiles
6	RP 2-1/4	S 3-1/4	B - 3-1/8			7/8		Rails
3	B - 3-1/8		16-7/8			RP 9/16	S 1/4	Panels
DRAWERS								
3	5-1/8		B + 5/8			3/4		Drawer Fronts
6	4-1/8		‡ B - 1/4	# B - 1-1/16		1/2		Front & Back Ends
6	4-1/8		18			1/2		Drawer Sides
3	‡ B - 3/4	# B - 1-9/16	17-5/8			1/4		Plywood Bottoms

* = Butt Joint   b = 1-3/4″ & 1-7/8″ Thick Ends   # = Side Mount Drawer Slide
** = Dado & Lip Joint   c = 2-7/8″ Thick Ends   RP = Raised Panel Door
a = 2-3/4″ Thick Ends   ‡ = Monorail Drawer Slide   S = Spanish Door

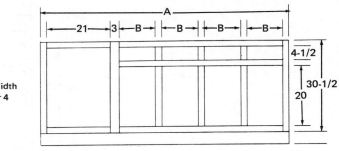

A = Cabinet Width
B = A − 34″ ÷ 4

LCB-4 84″ to 96″ four-door left-hand corner base cabinet.

No.	Width (″)		Length (″)			Thickness (″)		Part
FACE PLATE								
2	2		30-1/2			3/4		Stiles
2	2		22-1/2			3/4		Rails
3	2		A − 26-1/2			3/4		Rails
3	2		21-1/2			3/4		Mulls
3	2		6			3/4		Mulls
1	3		30-1/2			3/4		Mull
CABINET WITH BUTT OR DADO & LIP JOINT								
	*	**						
2	23-1/4	23-1/2	34-1/2			3/4		Base Ends
1	23		A − 7/8			3/4		Bottom
1	23-7/8		A − 5/8			1/4		Back
1	7		A − 1-5/8			3/4		Nailing Strip
1	4		A			3/4		Toe Board
CABINET WITH LOCK JOINT								
2	23-15/16		34-1/2			3/4 or 7/8		Base Ends
			a	b	c			
1	23		A − 1-1/16	A − 1-5/16	A − 1-9/16	3/4		Bottom
1	23-7/8		A − 3/8	A − 5/8	A − 7/8	1/4		Back
1	7		A − 1-13/16			3/4		Nailing Strip
1	4		A			3/4		Toe Board
DOORS								
4	B + 5/8		20-5/8			3/4		Plywood Doors or
4	B + 5/8		20-5/8			7/8		Raised Panel or Spanish Doors
RAISED PANEL OR SPANISH DOOR PARTS								
8	2-1/4		20-5/8			7/8		Stiles
	RP	S						
8	2-1/4	3-1/4	B − 3-1/8			7/8		Rails
						RP	S	
4	B − 3-1/8		16-7/8			9/16	1/4	Panels
DRAWERS								
4	5-1/8		B + 5/8			3/4		Drawer Fronts
			‡	#				
8	4-1/8		B − 1/4	B − 1-1/16		1/2		Front & Back Ends
8	4-1/8		18			1/2		Drawer Sides
	‡	#						
4	B − 3/4	B − 1-9/16	17-5/8			1/4		Plywood Bottoms

* = Butt Joint b = 1-3/4″ & 1-7/8″ Thick Ends # = Side Mount Drawer Slide
** = Dado & Lip Joint c = 2-7/8″ Thick Ends RP = Raised Panel Door
a = 2-3/4″ Thick Ends ‡ = Monorail Drawer Slide S = Spanish Door

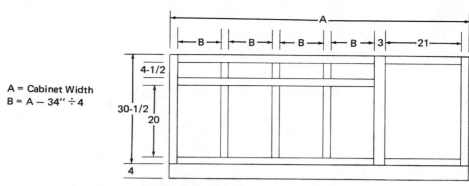

A = Cabinet Width
B = A − 34″ ÷ 4

RCB-4 84″ to 96″ four-door right-hand corner base cabinet.

No.	Width (″)		Length (″)			Thickness (″)		Part
FACE PLATE								
2	2		30-1/2			3/4		Stiles
2	2		22-1/2			3/4		Rails
3	2		A - 26-1/2			3/4		Rails
3	2		21-1/2			3/4		Mulls
3	2		6			3/4		Mulls
1	3		30-1/2			3/4		Mull
CABINET WITH BUTT OR DADO & LIP JOINT								
	*	**						
2	23-1/4	23-1/2	34-1/2			3/4		Base Ends
1	23		A - 7/8			3/4		Bottom
1	23-7/8		A - 5/8			1/4		Back
1	7		A - 1-5/8			3/4		Nailing Strip
1	4		A			3/4		Toe Board
CABINET WITH LOCK JOINT								
2	23-15/16		34-1/2			3/4 or 7/8		Base Ends
			a	b	c			
1	23		A - 1-1/16	A - 1-5/16	A - 1-9/16	3/4		Bottom
1	23-7/8		A - 3/8	A - 5/8	A - 7/8	1/4		Back
1	7		A - 1-13/16			3/4		Nailing Strip
1	4		A			3/4		Toe Board
DOORS								
4	B + 5/8		20-5/8			3/4		Plywood Doors or
4	B + 5/8		20-5/8			7/8		Raised Panel or Spanish Doors
RAISED PANEL OR SPANISH DOOR PARTS								
8	2-1/4		20-5/8			7/8		Stiles
	RP	S						
8	2-1/4	3-1/4	B - 3-1/8			7/8		Rails
						RP	S	
4	B - 3-1/8		16-7/8			9/16	1/4	Panels
DRAWERS								
4	5-1/8		B + 5/8			3/4		Drawer Fronts
			‡		#			
8	4-1/8		B - 1/4		B - 1-1/16	1/2		Front & Back Ends
8	4-1/8		18			1/2		Drawer Sides
	‡	#						
4	B - 3/4	B - 1-9/16	17-5/8			1/4		Plywood Bottoms

* = Butt Joint
** = Dado & Lip Joint
a = 2-3/4″ Thick Ends
b = 1-3/4″ & 1-7/8″ Thick Ends
c = 2-7/8″ Thick Ends
‡ = Monorail Drawer Slide
\# = Side Mount Drawer Slide
RP = Raised Panel Door
S = Spanish Door

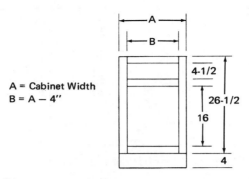

A = Cabinet Width
B = A − 4"

V-1 21" to 27" left-or-right-hand one sink, one door, no drawer vanity.

No.	Width (")		Length (")	Thickness (")		Part
FACE PLATE						
2	2		26-1/2	3/4		Stiles
3	2		A − 2-1/2	3/4		Rails
CABINET WITH BUTT OR DADO & LIP JOINT						
2	* 20-1/4	** 20-1/2	30-1/2	3/4		Vanity Ends
1	20		A − 7/8	3/4		Bottom
1	23-7/8		A − 5/8	1/4		Back
1	7		A − 1-5/8	3/4		Nailing Strip
1	4		A	3/4		Toe Board
CABINET WITH LOCK JOINT						
2	20-15/16		30-1/2	3/4		Vanity Ends
1	20		A − 1-1/16	3/4		Bottom
1	23-7/8		A − 3/8	1/4		Back
1	7		A − 1-13/16	3/4		Nailing Strip
1	4		A	3/4		Toe Board
DOOR						
1	B + 5/8		16-5/8	3/4		Plywood Door or
1	B + 5/8		16-5/8	7/8		Raised Panel or Spanish Door
RAISED PANEL OR SPANISH DOOR PARTS						
2	2-1/4		16-5/8	7/8		Stiles
2	RP 2-1/4	S 3-1/4	B − 3-1/8	7/8		Rails
1	B − 3-1/8		12-7/8	RP 9/16	S 1/4	Panel
GRILL						
1	5-1/8		B + 5/8	3/4		Grill

* = Butt Joint   RP = Raised Panel Door
** = Dado & Lip Joint   S = Spanish Door

174

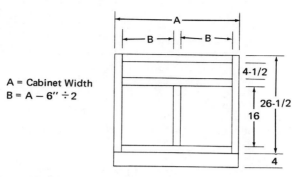

A = Cabinet Width
B = A − 6″ ÷ 2

4-1/2
26-1/2
16
4

V-2 27″ to 33″ one sink, two doors, no drawer vanity.

No.	Width (″)		Length (″)	Thickness (″)		Part
FACE PLATE						
2	2		26-1/2	3/4		Stiles
3	2		A - 2-1/2	3/4		Rails
1	2		17-1/2	3/4		Mull
CABINET WITH BUTT OR DADO & LIP JOINT						
	*	**				
2	20-1/4	20-1/2	30-1/2	3/4		Vanity Ends
1	20		A - 7/8	3/4		Bottom
1	23-7/8		A - 5/8	1/4		Back
1	7		A - 1-5/8	3/4		Nailing Strip
1	4		A	3/4		Toe Board
CABINET WITH LOCK JOINT						
2	20-15/16		30-1/2	3/4		Vanity Ends
1	20		A - 1-1/16	3/4		Bottom
1	23-7/8		A - 3/8	1/4		Back
1	7		A - 1-13/16	3/4		Nailing Strip
1	4		A	3/4		Toe Board
DOORS						
2	B + 5/8		16-5/8	3/4		Plywood Doors or
2	B + 5/8		16-5/8	7/8		Raised Panel or Spanish Doors
RAISED PANEL OR SPANISH DOOR PARTS						
4	2-1/4		16-5/8	7/8		Stiles
	RP	S				
4	2-1/4	3-1/4	B - 3-1/8	7/8		Rails
				RP	S	
2	B - 3-1/8		12-7/8	9/16	1/4	Panels
GRILL						
1	5-1/8		A - 3-3/8	3/4		Grill

* = Butt Joint   RP = Raised Panel Door
** = Dado & Lip Joint   S = Spanish Door

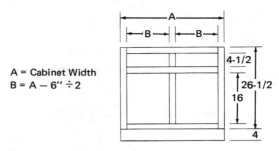

A = Cabinet Width
B = A — 6″ ÷ 2

V1D-2 36″ to 48″ left-or-right-hand one sink, two doors, one-drawer vanity.

No.	Width (″)		Length (″)		Thickness (″)		Part
			FACE PLATE				
2	2		26-1/2		3/4		Stiles
3	2		A - 2-1/2		3/4		Rails
1	2		17-1/2		3/4		Mull
1	2		6		3/4		Mull
			CABINET WITH BUTT OR DADO & LIP JOINT				
	*	**					
2	20-1/4	20-1/2	30-1/2		3/4		Vanity Ends
1	20		A - 7/8		3/4		Bottom
1	23-7/8		A - 5/8		1/4		Back
1	7		A - 1-5/8		3/4		Nailing Strip
1	4		A		3/4		Toe Board
			CABINET WITH LOCK JOINT				
2	20-15/16		30-1/2		3/4		Vanity Ends
1	20		A - 1-1/16		3/4		Bottom
1	23-7/8		A - 3/8		1/4		Back
1	7		A - 1-13/16		3/4		Nailing Strip
1	4		A		3/4		Toe Board
			DOORS				
2	B + 5/8		16-5/8		3/4		Plywood Doors or
2	B + 5/8		16-5/8		7/8		Raised Panel or Spanish Doors
			RAISED PANEL OR SPANISH DOOR PARTS				
4	2-1/4		16-5/8		7/8		Stiles
	RP	S					
4	2-1/4	3-1/4	B - 3-1/8		7/8		Rails
					RP	S	
2	B - 3-1/8		12-7/8		9/16	1/4	Panels
			GRILLS & DRAWERS				
1	5-1/8		B + 5/8		3/4		Grill
1	5-1/8		B + 5/8		3/4		Drawer Front
			‡	#			
2	4-1/8		B - 1/4	B - 1-1/16	1/2		Front & Back Ends
2	4-1/8		18		1/2		Drawer Sides
	‡	#					
1	B - 3/4	B - 1-9/16	17-5/8		1/4		Plywood Bottom

```
 *  = Butt Joint            ‡ = Monorail Drawer Slide     RP = Raised Panel Door
 ** = Dado & Lip Joint      # = Side Mount Drawer Slide    S = Spanish Door
```

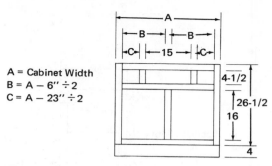

A = Cabinet Width
B = A − 6" ÷ 2
C = A − 23" ÷ 2

V2D-2 33" to 48" one sink, two doors, two-drawer vanity.

No.	Width (")		Length (")		Thickness (")		Part
			FACE PLATE				
2	2		26-1/2		3/4		Stiles
3	2		A - 2-1/2		3/4		Rails
1	2		17-1/2		3/4		Mull
2	2		6		3/4		Mulls
			CABINET WITH BUTT OR DADO & LIP JOINT				
	*	**					
2	20-1/4	20-1/2	30-1/2		3/4		Vanity Ends
1	20		A - 7/8		3/4		Bottom
1	23-7/8		A - 5/8		1/4		Back
1	7		A - 1-5/8		3/4		Nailing Strip
1	4		A		3/4		Toe Board
			CABINET WITH LOCK JOINT				
2	20-15/16		30-1/2		3/4		Vanity Ends
1	20		A - 1-1/16		3/4		Bottom
1	23-7/8		A - 3/8		1/4		Back
1	7		A - 1-13/16		3/4		Nailing Strip
1	4		A		3/4		Toe Board
			DOORS				
2	B + 5/8		16-5/8		3/4		Plywood Doors or
2	B + 5/8		16-5/8		7/8		Raised Panel or Spanish Doors
			RAISED PANEL OR SPANISH DOOR PARTS				
4	2-1/4		16-5/8		7/8		Stiles
	RP	S					
4	2-1/4	3-1/4	B - 3-1/8		7/8		Rails
					RP	S	
2	B - 3-1/8		12-7/8		9/16	1/4	Panels
			GRILLS & DRAWERS				
1	5-1/8		15-5/8		3/4		Grill
2	5-1/8		C + 5/8		3/4		Drawer Fronts
			‡	#			
4	4-1/8		C - 1/4	C - 1-1/16	1/2		Front & Back Ends
4	4-1/8		18		1/2		Drawer Sides
	‡	#					
2	C - 3/4	C - 1-9/16	17-5/8		1/4		Plywood Bottoms

* = Butt Joint ‡ = Monorail Drawer Slide RP = Raised Panel Door
** = Dado & Lip Joint # = Side Mount Drawer Slide S = Spanish Door

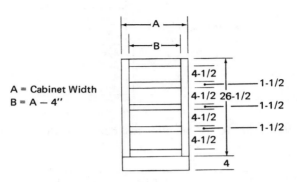

A = Cabinet Width
B = A − 4''

SD 12″ to 24″ stack of drawers vanity.

No.	Width ('')		Length ('')		Thickness ('')	Part
FACE PLATE						
2	2		26-1/2		3/4	Stiles
2	2		A - 2-1/2		3/4	Rails
3	1-1/2		A - 2-1/2		3/4	Rails
CABINET WITH BUTT OR DADO & LIP JOINT						
	*	**				
2	20-1/4	20-1/2	30-1/2		3/4	Vanity Ends
1	20		A - 7/8		3/4	Bottom
1	23-7/8		A - 5/8		1/4	Back
1	7		A - 1-5/8		3/4	Nailing Strip
1	4		A		3/4	Toe Board
CABINET WITH LOCK JOINT						
2	20-15/16		30-1/2		3/4	Vanity Ends
1	20		A - 1-1/16		3/4	Bottom
1	23-7/8		A - 3/8		1/4	Back
1	7		A - 1-13/16		3/4	Nailing Strip
1	4		A		3/4	Toe Board
DRAWERS						
4	5-1/8		B + 5/8		3/4	Drawer Fronts
			‡	#		
8	4-1/8		B - 1/4	B - 1-1/16	1/2	Front & Back Ends
8	4-1/8		18		1/2	Drawer Sides
	‡	#				
4	B - 3/4	B - 1-9/16	17-5/8		1/4	Plywood Bottoms

* = Butt Joint   ‡ = Monorail Drawer Slide
** = Dado & Lip Joint   # = Side Mount Drawer Slide

178

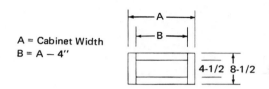

A = Cabinet Width
B = A — 4"

4-1/2 8-1/2

KD 21" to 27" one-drawer knee space for vanity.

No.	Width ('')		Length ('')		Thickness ('')	Part
FACE PLATE						
2	2		8 - 1/2		3/4	Stiles
2	2		A - 2-1/2		3/4	Rails
CABINET WITH BUTT OR DADO & LIP JOINT						
	*	**				
2	20-1/4	20-1/4	8-1/2		3/4	Vanity Ends
1	8-1/2		A - 1-5/8		3/4	Back
CABINET WITH LOCK JOINT						
2	20-15/16		8-1/2		3/4	Vanity Ends
1	8-1/2		A - 1-13/16		3/4	Back
DRAWER						
1	5-1/8		B + 5/8		3/4	Drawer Front
2	4-1/8		‡ B - 1/4	# B - 1-1/16	1/2	Front & Back Ends
2	4-1/8		18		1/2	Drawer Sides
1	‡ B - 3/4	# B - 1-9/16	17-5/8		1/4	Plywood Bottom

* = Butt Joint   ‡ = Monorail Drawer Slide
** = Dado & Lip Joint   # = Side Mount Drawer Slide

chapter 12

CABINET INSTALLATION

During all the different stages of the cabinet construction, the ultimate goal is to install the cabinet in the space for which it was built.

Where cabinetmaking is the building of a cabinet or several cabinets, cabinet installation is the completion of a kitchen. Cabinet installation is just as important as building the cabinet. A poor installation job will make a cabinet of superb craftsmanship look bad; vice versa, a good installation job will make a mediocre built cabinet look good.

Wall cabinets should be installed before the 24" deep base cabinets; otherwise it is difficult to get close enough to install the wall cabinets.

Base cabinets, including the laminated plastic top, are 36" high. The distance between the plastic top and the bottom of the wall cabinet is 18", thus making the distance from the floor to the bottom of the wall cabinet 54" (see Fig. 12-1).

The wall and base cabinets should be installed in the sequence in which they are shown in Fig. 12-2.

The wall cabinets that go on each side of a window (1 and 2) should be installed first. These cabinets should fit next to the window trim.

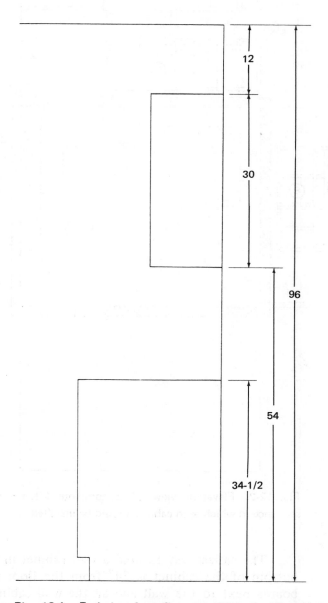

Fig. 12-1 End view from floor to ceiling of wall and base cabinets, showing dimensions.

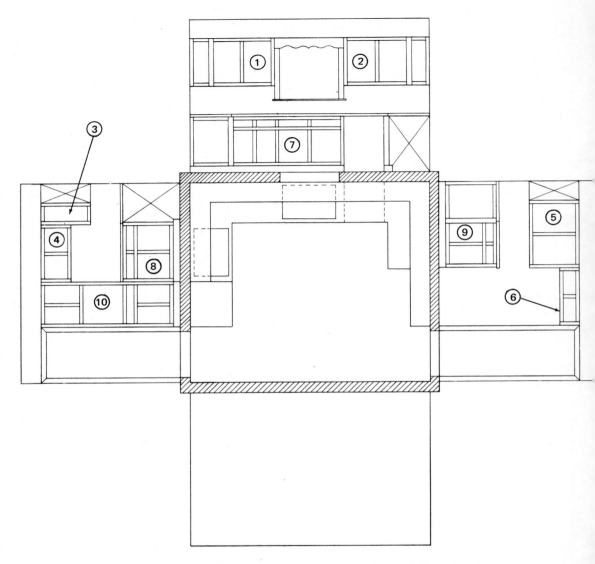

Fig. 12-2 Elevation view of a complete kitchen showing the sequence in which each cabinet should be installed.

The easiest way to hold a wall cabinet in position where the bottom of the cabinet is 54″ from the floor is to hold two 54″ boards next to the wall and sit the wall cabinet on top of them (see Fig. 12-3). This will eliminate measuring each cabinet separately.

Both wall and base cabinets are fastened to the wall with wood screws that extend through the backs of the cabinet into the wall. These screws must be fastened to the studs in the wall because wallboard or plaster is not strong enough to hold a cabinet to the wall.

Studs are the vertical pieces of a wall on which the outside sheathing and the inside wallboard or plaster are attached. Studs are usually 16″ on centers but since they are covered, they must usually be found by tapping on the wall.

A wood screw should be used at the top and bottom and in the same location of every wall stud for fastening the wall cabinet

Fig. 12-3   A wall cabinet sitting on two 54″ boards.

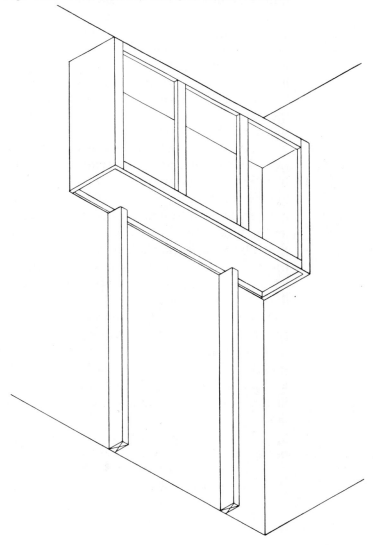

to the wall. Screws are used only at the tops and in the same location of the wall studs for fastening the base cabinets to the walls.

After the wall and base cabinets have been fastened to the walls, place the laminated plastic top in position on top of the base cabinets for locating the backsplash.

If a 4″ high backsplash is used, it should fit flush with the wall and not with the back edge of the top. This will eliminate spaces between the top and the wall if the wall is not straight.

Place the backsplash on the top, push it back toward the wall, and make a pencil mark on the top where the backsplash should go. Use the same procedure for drilling holes in the top and attaching the backsplash to the top that was used in Fig. 7-27.

The top can be fastened to the base cabinets by running wood screws up through the corner blocks in the base cabinet into the bottom surface of the plastic top.

If an 18″ high or full backsplash is used, the cutouts for the electrical outlets on the wall must be made before the backsplash is fastened to the top.

To avoid making errors in determining the cutouts for the electrical outlets, do not attempt to measure along the wall and transfer these measurements on the backsplash. Draw a vertical line on each side of the outlet up to the bottom of the wall cabinet. Draw a horizontal line at the top and bottom of the outlet (see Fig. 12-4).

Place the backsplash in position and make a pencil mark on the backsplash that is in line with the pencil mark from the outlet up to the bottom of the wall cabinet. Use a framing square and draw two pencil lines from the pencil marks down the backsplash. Measure from the wall cabinet down to the horizontal lines above and below the electrical outlet and make a pencil mark at the same measurement on the backsplash. Drill a hole in the backsplash in the center of the place where the outlet opening is to be located and cut out the opening with a sabre saw. The pencil lines on the plastic backsplash can easily be wiped off with a damp cloth.

Use the same procedure for attaching the 18″ high or full backsplash to the top that was used in Fig. 7-29.

The top is fastened to the base cabinets just like the top with the 4″ high backsplash, and that is by running wood screws up

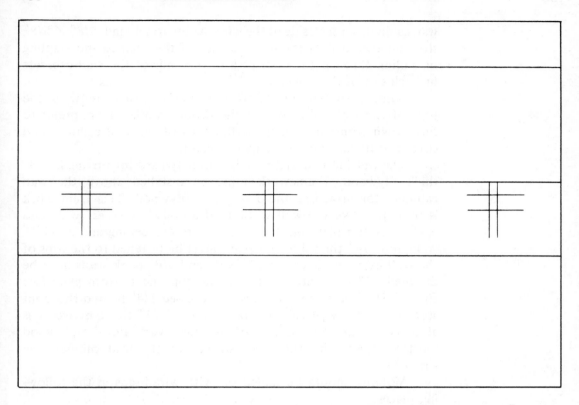

Fig. 12-4   Determining cutout for the electrical outlets on an 18″
high backsplash.

through the base cabinet corner blocks into the bottom surface of
the plastic top.

The top of the 18″ high or full backsplash is fastened to
the wall by nailing 4d finishing nails about 1/4″ down from the
top edge of the backsplash into the wall studs. These nails are
later covered with the molding.

After the top has been fastened to the base cabinets, the
oven cabinet can be fastened to the wall and the ends of the
wall and base cabinets that butt into it. Since the plastic top
butts into the end of the oven cabinet, it is almost impossible to
fit the top in position if the oven cabinet has already been fastened
to the wall and the wall base cabinets.

The valance above the window is fastened to the top of the

wall cabinets on each side of the window by attaching a 5/8" × 5/8" strip on each end of the back surface of the valance and stapling or nailing through these strips into the ends of the wall cabinets on each side of the window.

Some customers prefer to leave the 12" space between the tops of the wall cabinets and the ceiling, while others prefer to furr down from the ceiling to the tops of the wall cabinets and cover this furring with wallpaper or paint.

The outside material that is normally used for furring is 1/4" thick plywood. Framework must be installed above the wall cabinets for attaching the 1/4" thick plywood. This framework is built just like the wall sections of a house. A 1-1/2" wide and 3/4" thick top plate must be fastened to the ceiling and a 1-1/2" wide and 3/4" thick bottom plate must be fastened to the tops of the wall cabinets. Short 1-1/2" wide and 3/4" thick studs must be fastened 16" on centers between the top and bottom plate (see Fig. 12-5). This framework must be recessed 1/4" behind the front surface of the wall cabinets because the 1/4" thick plywood is attached to the front surface of the framework and the plywood must be flush with the front surface of the wall cabinet (see Fig. 12-6).

Molding should be nailed on with wire brads in the following places:

1. Along the surface of the furring next to the ceiling.
2. Between the furring and the tops of the wall cabinets.
3. Along the back edges of the wall and base cabinets and next to the wall.
4. Along the top surface of the full backsplash and the bottoms of the wall cabinets.
5. To cover the edges of the full backsplash.

The end of one piece of molding should never butt into the end or edge of another piece of molding. Every joint should be mitered at 45 degrees. Since the molding is prestained at the same time as the cabinets, all miter cuts should be cut with a power miter box using a fine-tooth saw blade (see Fig. 12-7).

The person doing the cabinet installation is also expected to install the kitchen appliances. The built-in oven and the dishwasher are installed in the openings that were left for them but a

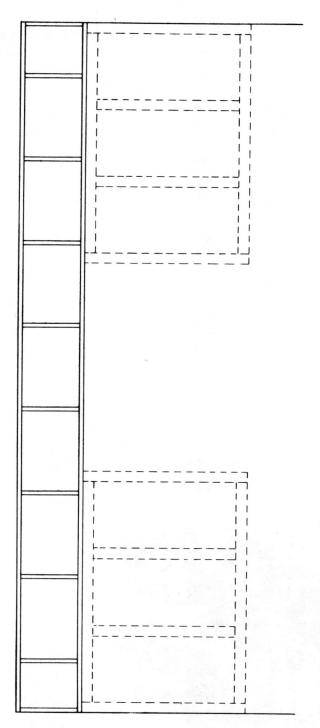

Fig. 12-5 Front view of framework to support furring above wall cabinets.

Fig. 12-6   End view of framework
for supporting furring.

Fig. 12-7   Power miter box.

cutout must be made in the plastic top for the sink and the surface unit. Some cabinetmakers prefer to make the sink and surface unit cutouts at the shop, while others prefer to make the cutouts at the job site. A template or the exact dimensions are usually furnished for the exact size of the cutouts.

From the time the first piece of rough lumber is planed until the cabinet is installed, the cabinetmaker should always strive for perfection.

INDEX